Mometrix
TEST PREPARATION

Secrets of the

ACE

Group Fitness Instructor
Exam Study Guide

DEAR FUTURE EXAM SUCCESS STORY

First of all, **THANK YOU** for purchasing Mometrix study materials!

Second, congratulations! You are one of the few determined test-takers who are committed to doing whatever it takes to excel on your exam. **You have come to the right place.** We developed these study materials with one goal in mind: to deliver you the information you need in a format that's concise and easy to use.

In addition to optimizing your guide for the content of the test, we've outlined our recommended steps for breaking down the preparation process into small, attainable goals so you can make sure you stay on track.

We've also analyzed the entire test-taking process, identifying the most common pitfalls and showing how you can overcome them and be ready for any curveball the test throws you.

Standardized testing is one of the biggest obstacles on your road to success, which only increases the importance of doing well in the high-pressure, high-stakes environment of test day. Your results on this test could have a significant impact on your future, and this guide provides the information and practical advice to help you achieve your full potential on test day.

Your success is our success

We would love to hear from you! If you would like to share the story of your exam success or if you have any questions or comments in regard to our products, please contact us at **800-673-8175** or **support@mometrix.com**.

Thanks again for your business and we wish you continued success!

Sincerely,
The Mometrix Test Preparation Team

Need more help? Check out our flashcards at:
http://MometrixFlashcards.com/GroupFitness

TABLE OF CONTENTS

Introduction

Thank you for purchasing this resource! You have made the choice to prepare yourself for a test that could have a huge impact on your future, and this guide is designed to help you be fully ready for test day. Obviously, it's important to have a solid understanding of the test material, but you also need to be prepared for the unique environment and stressors of the test, so that you can perform to the best of your abilities.

For this purpose, the first section that appears in this guide is the **Secret Keys**. We've devoted countless hours to meticulously researching what works and what doesn't, and we've boiled down our findings to the five most impactful steps you can take to improve your performance on the test. We start at the beginning with study planning and move through the preparation process, all the way to the testing strategies that will help you get the most out of what you know when you're finally sitting in front of the test.

We recommend that you start preparing for your test as far in advance as possible. However, if you've bought this guide as a last-minute study resource and only have a few days before your test, we recommend that you skip over the first two Secret Keys since they address a long-term study plan.

If you struggle with **test anxiety**, we strongly encourage you to check out our recommendations for how you can overcome it. Test anxiety is a formidable foe, but it can be beaten, and we want to make sure you have the tools you need to defeat it.

Secret Key 1: Plan Big, Study Small

There's a lot riding on your performance. If you want to ace this test, you're going to need to keep your skills sharp and the material fresh in your mind. You need a plan that lets you review everything you need to know while still fitting in your schedule. We'll break this strategy down into three categories.

Information Organization

Start with the information you already have: the official test outline. From this, you can make a complete list of all the concepts you need to cover before the test. Organize these concepts into groups that can be studied together, and create a list of any related vocabulary you need to learn so you can brush up on any difficult terms. You'll want to keep this vocabulary list handy once you actually start studying since you may need to add to it along the way.

Time Management

Once you have your set of study concepts, decide how to spread them out over the time you have left before the test. Break your study plan into small, clear goals so you have a manageable task for each day and know exactly what you're doing. Then just focus on one small step at a time. When you manage your time this way, you don't need to spend hours at a time studying. Studying a small block of content for a short period each day helps you retain information better and avoid stressing over how much you have left to do. You can relax knowing that you have a plan to cover everything in time. In order for this strategy to be effective though, you have to start studying early and stick to your schedule. Avoid the exhaustion and futility that comes from last-minute cramming!

Study Environment

The environment you study in has a big impact on your learning. Studying in a coffee shop, while probably more enjoyable, is not likely to be as fruitful as studying in a quiet room. It's important to keep distractions to a minimum. You're only planning to study for a short block of time, so make the most of it. Don't pause to check your phone or get up to find a snack. It's also important to **avoid multitasking**. Research has consistently shown that multitasking will make your studying dramatically less effective. Your study area should also be comfortable and well-lit so you don't have the distraction of straining your eyes or sitting on an uncomfortable chair.

The time of day you study is also important. You want to be rested and alert. Don't wait until just before bedtime. Study when you'll be most likely to comprehend and remember. Even better, if you know what time of day your test will be, set that time aside for study. That way your brain will be used to working on that subject at that specific time and you'll have a better chance of recalling information.

Finally, it can be helpful to team up with others who are studying for the same test. Your actual studying should be done in as isolated an environment as possible, but the work of organizing the information and setting up the study plan can be divided up. In between study sessions, you can discuss with your teammates the concepts that you're all studying and quiz each other on the details. Just be sure that your teammates are as serious about the test as you are. If you find that your study time is being replaced with social time, you might need to find a new team.

Secret Key 2: Make Your Studying Count

You're devoting a lot of time and effort to preparing for this test, so you want to be absolutely certain it will pay off. This means doing more than just reading the content and hoping you can remember it on test day. It's important to make every minute of study count. There are two main areas you can focus on to make your studying count.

Retention

It doesn't matter how much time you study if you can't remember the material. You need to make sure you are retaining the concepts. To check your retention of the information you're learning, try recalling it at later times with minimal prompting. Try carrying around flashcards and glance at one or two from time to time or ask a friend who's also studying for the test to quiz you.

To enhance your retention, look for ways to put the information into practice so that you can apply it rather than simply recalling it. If you're using the information in practical ways, it will be much easier to remember. Similarly, it helps to solidify a concept in your mind if you're not only reading it to yourself but also explaining it to someone else. Ask a friend to let you teach them about a concept you're a little shaky on (or speak aloud to an imaginary audience if necessary). As you try to summarize, define, give examples, and answer your friend's questions, you'll understand the concepts better and they will stay with you longer. Finally, step back for a big picture view and ask yourself how each piece of information fits with the whole subject. When you link the different concepts together and see them working together as a whole, it's easier to remember the individual components.

Finally, practice showing your work on any multi-step problems, even if you're just studying. Writing out each step you take to solve a problem will help solidify the process in your mind, and you'll be more likely to remember it during the test.

Modality

Modality simply refers to the means or method by which you study. Choosing a study modality that fits your own individual learning style is crucial. No two people learn best in exactly the same way, so it's important to know your strengths and use them to your advantage.

4

For example, if you learn best by visualization, focus on visualizing a concept in your mind and draw an image or a diagram. Try color-coding your notes, illustrating them, or creating symbols that will trigger your mind to recall a learned concept. If you learn best by hearing or discussing information, find a study partner who learns the same way or read aloud to yourself. Think about how to put the information in your own words. Imagine that you are giving a lecture on the topic and record yourself so you can listen to it later.

For any learning style, flashcards can be helpful. Organize the information so you can take advantage of spare moments to review. Underline key words or phrases. Use different colors for different categories. Mnemonic devices (such as creating a short list in which every item starts with the same letter) can also help with retention. Find what works best for you and use it to store the information in your mind most effectively and easily.

Secret Key 3: Practice the Right Way

Your success on test day depends not only on how many hours you put into preparing, but also on whether you prepared the right way. It's good to check along the way to see if your studying is paying off. One of the most effective ways to do this is by taking practice tests to evaluate your progress. Practice tests are useful because they show exactly where you need to improve. Every time you take a practice test, pay special attention to these three groups of questions:

- The questions you got wrong
- The questions you had to guess on, even if you guessed right
- The questions you found difficult or slow to work through

This will show you exactly what your weak areas are, and where you need to devote more study time. Ask yourself why each of these questions gave you trouble. Was it because you didn't understand the material? Was it because you didn't remember the vocabulary? Do you need more repetitions on this type of question to build speed and confidence? Dig into those questions and figure out how you can strengthen your weak areas as you go back to review the material.

Additionally, many practice tests have a section explaining the answer choices. It can be tempting to read the explanation and think that you now have a good understanding of the concept. However, an explanation likely only covers part of the question's broader context. Even if the explanation makes perfect sense, **go back and investigate** every concept related to the question until you're positive you have a thorough understanding.

As you go along, keep in mind that the practice test is just that: practice. Memorizing these questions and answers will not be very helpful on the actual test because it is unlikely to have any of the same exact questions. If you only know the right answers to the sample questions, you won't be prepared for the real thing. **Study the concepts** until you understand them fully, and then you'll be able to answer any question that shows up on the test.

It's important to wait on the practice tests until you're ready. If you take a test on your first day of study, you may be overwhelmed by the amount of material covered and how much you need to learn. Work up to it gradually.

On test day, you'll need to be prepared for answering questions, managing your time, and using the test-taking strategies you've learned. It's a lot to balance, like a mental marathon that will have a big impact on your future. Like training for a marathon, you'll need to start slowly and work your way up. When test day arrives, you'll be ready.

6

Start with the strategies you've read in the first two Secret Keys—plan your course and study in the way that works best for you. If you have time, consider using multiple study resources to get different approaches to the same concepts. It can be helpful to see difficult concepts from more than one angle. Then find a good source for practice tests. Many times, the test website will suggest potential study resources or provide sample tests.

Practice Test Strategy

If you're able to find at least three practice tests, we recommend this strategy:

UNTIMED AND OPEN-BOOK PRACTICE

Take the first test with no time constraints and with your notes and study guide handy. Take your time and focus on applying the strategies you've learned.

TIMED AND OPEN-BOOK PRACTICE

Take the second practice test open-book as well, but set a timer and practice pacing yourself to finish in time.

TIMED AND CLOSED-BOOK PRACTICE

Take any other practice tests as if it were test day. Set a timer and put away your study materials. Sit at a table or desk in a quiet room, imagine yourself at the testing center, and answer questions as quickly and accurately as possible.

Keep repeating timed and closed-book tests on a regular basis until you run out of practice tests or it's time for the actual test. Your mind will be ready for the schedule and stress of test day, and you'll be able to focus on recalling the material you've learned.

Secret Key 4: Pace Yourself

Once you're fully prepared for the material on the test, your biggest challenge on test day will be managing your time. Just knowing that the clock is ticking can make you panic even if you have plenty of time left. Work on pacing yourself so you can build confidence against the time constraints of the exam. Pacing is a difficult skill to master, especially in a high-pressure environment, so **practice is vital**.

Set time expectations for your pace based on how much time is available. For example, if a section has 60 questions and the time limit is 30 minutes, you know you have to average 30 seconds or less per question in order to answer them all. Although 30 seconds is the hard limit, set 25 seconds per question as your goal, so you reserve extra time to spend on harder questions. When you budget extra time for the harder questions, you no longer have any reason to stress when those questions take longer to answer.

Don't let this time expectation distract you from working through the test at a calm, steady pace, but keep it in mind so you don't spend too much time on any one question. Recognize that taking extra time on one question you don't understand may keep you from answering two that you do understand later in the test. If your time limit for a question is up and you're still not sure of the answer, mark it and move on, and come back to it later if the time and the test format allow. If the testing format doesn't allow you to return to earlier questions, just make an educated guess; then put it out of your mind and move on.

On the easier questions, be careful not to rush. It may seem wise to hurry through them so you have more time for the challenging ones, but it's not worth missing one if you know the concept and just didn't take the time to read the question fully. Work efficiently but make sure you understand the question and have looked at all of the answer choices, since more than one may seem right at first.

Even if you're paying attention to the time, you may find yourself a little behind at some point. You should speed up to get back on track, but do so wisely. Don't panic; just take a few seconds less on each question until you're caught up. Don't guess without thinking, but do look through the answer choices and eliminate any you know are wrong. If you can get down to two choices, it is often worthwhile to guess from those. Once you've chosen an answer, move on and don't dwell on any that you skipped or had to hurry through. If a question was taking too long, chances are it was one of the harder ones, so you weren't as likely to get it right anyway.

On the other hand, if you find yourself getting ahead of schedule, it may be beneficial to slow down a little. The more quickly you work, the more likely you are to make a careless mistake that will affect your score. You've budgeted time for each question, so don't be afraid to spend that time. Practice an efficient but careful pace to get the most out of the time you have.

Secret Key 5: Have a Plan for Guessing

When you're taking the test, you may find yourself stuck on a question. Some of the answer choices seem better than others, but you don't see the one answer choice that is obviously correct. What do you do?

The scenario described above is very common, yet most test takers have not effectively prepared for it. Developing and practicing a plan for guessing may be one of the single most effective uses of your time as you get ready for the exam.

In developing your plan for guessing, there are three questions to address:

- When should you start the guessing process?
- How should you narrow down the choices?
- Which answer should you choose?

When to Start the Guessing Process

Unless your plan for guessing is to select C every time (which, despite its merits, is not what we recommend), you need to leave yourself enough time to apply your answer elimination strategies. Since you have a limited amount of time for each question, that means that if you're going to give yourself the best shot at guessing correctly, you have to decide quickly whether or not you will guess.

Of course, the best-case scenario is that you don't have to guess at all, so first, see if you can answer the question based on your knowledge of the subject and basic reasoning skills. Focus on the key words in the question and try to jog your memory of related topics. Give yourself a chance to bring the knowledge to mind, but once you realize that you don't have (or you can't access) the knowledge you need to answer the question, it's time to start the guessing process.

It's almost always better to start the guessing process too early than too late. It only takes a few seconds to remember something and answer the question from knowledge. Carefully eliminating wrong answer choices takes longer. Plus, going through the process of eliminating answer choices can actually help jog your memory.

Summary: Start the guessing process as soon as you decide that you can't answer the question based on your knowledge.

How to Narrow Down the Choices

The next chapter in this book (**Test-Taking Strategies**) includes a wide range of strategies for how to approach questions and how to look for answer choices to eliminate. You will definitely want to read those carefully, practice them, and figure out which ones work best for you. Here though, we're going to address a mindset rather than a particular strategy.

Your odds of guessing an answer correctly depend on how many options you are choosing from.

Number of options left	5	4	3	2	1
Odds of guessing correctly	20%	25%	33%	50%	100%

You can see from this chart just how valuable it is to be able to eliminate incorrect answers and make an educated guess, but there are two things that many test takers do that cause them to miss out on the benefits of guessing:

- Accidentally eliminating the correct answer
- Selecting an answer based on an impression

We'll look at the first one here, and the second one in the next section.

To avoid accidentally eliminating the correct answer, we recommend a thought exercise called **the $5 challenge**. In this challenge, you only eliminate an answer choice from contention if you are willing to bet $5 on it being wrong. Why $5? Five dollars is a small but not insignificant amount of money. It's an amount you could

afford to lose but wouldn't want to throw away. And while losing $5 once might not hurt too much, doing it twenty times will set you back $100. In the same way, each small decision you make—eliminating a choice here, guessing on a question there—won't by itself impact your score very much, but when you put them all together, they can make a big difference. By holding each answer choice elimination decision to a higher standard, you can reduce the risk of accidentally eliminating the correct answer.

The $5 challenge can also be applied in a positive sense: If you are willing to bet $5 that an answer choice *is* correct, go ahead and mark it as correct.

Summary: Only eliminate an answer choice if you are willing to bet $5 that it is wrong.

11

Which Answer to Choose

You're taking the test. You've run into a hard question and decided you'll have to guess. You've eliminated all the answer choices you're willing to bet $5 on. Now you have to pick an answer. Why do we even need to talk about this? Why can't you just pick whichever one you feel like when the time comes?

The answer to these questions is that if you don't come into the test with a plan, you'll rely on your impression to select an answer choice, and if you do that, you risk falling into a trap. The test writers know that everyone who takes their test will be guessing on some of the questions, so they intentionally write wrong answer choices to seem plausible. You still have to pick an answer though, and if the wrong answer choices are designed to look right, how can you ever be sure that you're not falling for their trap? The best solution we've found to this dilemma is to take the decision out of your hands entirely. Here is the process we recommend:

Once you've eliminated any choices that you are confident (willing to bet $5) are wrong, select the first remaining choice as your answer.

Whether you choose to select the first remaining choice, the second, or the last, the important thing is that you use some preselected standard. Using this approach guarantees that you will not be enticed into selecting an answer choice that looks right, because you are not basing your decision on how the answer choices look.

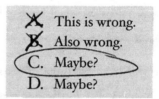

This is not meant to make you question your knowledge. Instead, it is to help you recognize the difference between your knowledge and your impressions. There's a huge difference between thinking an answer is right because of what you know, and thinking an answer is right because it looks or sounds like it should be right.

Summary: To ensure that your selection is appropriately random, make a predetermined selection from among all answer choices you have not eliminated.

Test-Taking Strategies

This section contains a list of test-taking strategies that you may find helpful as you work through the test. By taking what you know and applying logical thought, you can maximize your chances of answering any question correctly!

It is very important to realize that every question is different and every person is different: no single strategy will work on every question, and no single strategy will work for every person. That's why we've included all of them here, so you can try them out and determine which ones work best for different types of questions and which ones work best for you.

Question Strategies

⊘ READ CAREFULLY

Read the question and the answer choices carefully. Don't miss the question because you misread the terms. You have plenty of time to read each question thoroughly and make sure you understand what is being asked. Yet a happy medium must be attained, so don't waste too much time. You must read carefully and efficiently.

⊘ CONTEXTUAL CLUES

Look for contextual clues. If the question includes a word you are not familiar with, look at the immediate context for some indication of what the word might mean. Contextual clues can often give you all the information you need to decipher the meaning of an unfamiliar word. Even if you can't determine the meaning, you may be able to narrow down the possibilities enough to make a solid guess at the answer to the question.

⊘ PREFIXES

If you're having trouble with a word in the question or answer choices, try dissecting it. Take advantage of every clue that the word might include. Prefixes can be a huge help. Usually, they allow you to determine a basic meaning. *Pre-* means before, *post-* means after, *pro-* is positive, *de-* is negative. From prefixes, you can get an idea of the general meaning of the word and try to put it into context.

⊘ HEDGE WORDS

Watch out for critical hedge words, such as *likely, may, can, sometimes, often, almost, mostly, usually, generally, rarely,* and *sometimes*. Question writers insert these hedge phrases to cover every possibility. Often an answer choice will be wrong simply because it leaves no room for exception. Be on guard for answer choices that have definitive words such as *exactly* and *always*.

13

⊘ SWITCHBACK WORDS

Stay alert for *switchbacks*. These are the words and phrases frequently used to alert you to shifts in thought. The most common switchback words are *but*, *although*, and *however*. Others include *nevertheless, on the other hand, even though, while, in spite of, despite,* and *regardless of.* Switchback words are important to catch because they can change the direction of the question or an answer choice.

⊘ FACE VALUE

When in doubt, use common sense. Accept the situation in the problem at face value. Don't read too much into it. These problems will not require you to make wild assumptions. If you have to go beyond creativity and warp time or space in order to have an answer choice fit the question, then you should move on and consider the other answer choices. These are normal problems rooted in reality. The applicable relationship or explanation may not be readily apparent, but it is there for you to figure out. Use your common sense to interpret anything that isn't clear.

Answer Choice Strategies

⊘ ANSWER SELECTION

The most thorough way to pick an answer choice is to identify and eliminate wrong answers until only one is left, then confirm it is the correct answer. Sometimes an answer choice may immediately seem right, but be careful. The test writers will usually put more than one reasonable answer choice on each question, so take a second to read all of them and make sure that the other choices are not equally obvious. As long as you have time left, it is better to read every answer choice than to pick the first one that looks right without checking the others.

⊘ ANSWER CHOICE FAMILIES

An answer choice family consists of two (in rare cases, three) answer choices that are very similar in construction and cannot all be true at the same time. If you see two answer choices that are direct opposites or parallels, one of them is usually the correct answer. For instance, if one answer choice says that quantity x increases and another either says that quantity x decreases (opposite) or says that quantity y increases (parallel), then those answer choices would fall into the same family. An answer choice that doesn't match the construction of the answer choice family is more likely to be incorrect. Most questions will not have answer choice families, but when they do appear, you should be prepared to recognize them.

⊘ ELIMINATE ANSWERS

Eliminate answer choices as soon as you realize they are wrong, but make sure you consider all possibilities. If you are eliminating answer choices and realize that the last one you are left with is also wrong, don't panic. Start over and consider each choice again. There may be something you missed the first time that you will realize on the second pass.

14

⊘ Avoid Fact Traps

Don't be distracted by an answer choice that is factually true but doesn't answer the question. You are looking for the choice that answers the question. Stay focused on what the question is asking for so you don't accidentally pick an answer that is true but incorrect. Always go back to the question and make sure the answer choice you've selected actually answers the question and is not merely a true statement.

⊘ Extreme Statements

In general, you should avoid answers that put forth extreme actions as standard practice or proclaim controversial ideas as established fact. An answer choice that states the "process should be used in certain situations, if…" is much more likely to be correct than one that states the "process should be discontinued completely." The first is a calm rational statement and doesn't even make a definitive, uncompromising stance, using a hedge word *if* to provide wiggle room, whereas the second choice is far more extreme.

⊘ Benchmark

As you read through the answer choices and you come across one that seems to answer the question well, mentally select that answer choice. This is not your final answer, but it's the one that will help you evaluate the other answer choices. The one that you selected is your benchmark or standard for judging each of the other answer choices. Every other answer choice must be compared to your benchmark. That choice is correct until proven otherwise by another answer choice beating it. If you find a better answer, then that one becomes your new benchmark. Once you've decided that no other choice answers the question as well as your benchmark, you have your final answer.

⊘ Predict the Answer

Before you even start looking at the answer choices, it is often best to try to predict the answer. When you come up with the answer on your own, it is easier to avoid distractions and traps because you will know exactly what to look for. The right answer choice is unlikely to be word-for-word what you came up with, but it should be a close match. Even if you are confident that you have the right answer, you should still take the time to read each option before moving on.

General Strategies

⊘ Tough Questions

If you are stumped on a problem or it appears too hard or too difficult, don't waste time. Move on! Remember though, if you can quickly check for obviously incorrect answer choices, your chances of guessing correctly are greatly improved. Before you completely give up, at least try to knock out a couple of possible answers. Eliminate what you can and then guess at the remaining answer choices before moving on.

⊘ CHECK YOUR WORK

Since you will probably not know every term listed and the answer to every question, it is important that you get credit for the ones that you do know. Don't miss any questions through careless mistakes. If at all possible, try to take a second to look back over your answer selection and make sure you've selected the correct answer choice and haven't made a costly careless mistake (such as marking an answer choice that you didn't mean to mark). This quick double check should more than pay for itself in caught mistakes for the time it costs.

⊘ PACE YOURSELF

It's easy to be overwhelmed when you're looking at a page full of questions; your mind is confused and full of random thoughts, and the clock is ticking down faster than you would like. Calm down and maintain the pace that you have set for yourself. Especially as you get down to the last few minutes of the test, don't let the small numbers on the clock make you panic. As long as you are on track by monitoring your pace, you are guaranteed to have time for each question.

⊘ DON'T RUSH

It is very easy to make errors when you are in a hurry. Maintaining a fast pace in answering questions is pointless if it makes you miss questions that you would have gotten right otherwise. Test writers like to include distracting information and wrong answers that seem right. Taking a little extra time to avoid careless mistakes can make all the difference in your test score. Find a pace that allows you to be confident in the answers that you select.

⊘ KEEP MOVING

Panicking will not help you pass the test, so do your best to stay calm and keep moving. Taking deep breaths and going through the answer elimination steps you practiced can help to break through a stress barrier and keep your pace.

Final Notes

The combination of a solid foundation of content knowledge and the confidence that comes from practicing your plan for applying that knowledge is the key to maximizing your performance on test day. As your foundation of content knowledge is built up and strengthened, you'll find that the strategies included in this chapter become more and more effective in helping you quickly sift through the distractions and traps of the test to isolate the correct answer.

Now that you're preparing to move forward into the test content chapters of this book, be sure to keep your goal in mind. As you read, think about how you will be able to apply this information on the test. If you've already seen sample questions for the test and you have an idea of the question format and style, try to come up with questions of your own that you can answer based on what you're reading. This will give you valuable practice applying your knowledge in the same ways you can expect to on test day.

Good luck and good studying!

Exercise Programming and Class Design

WARM-UP

There are a few different reasons why every workout should begin with a warm up session. For one thing, it is healthier for the heart to have a gradual introduction to exercise. If the heart is asked to go from a state of rest to a state of major exertion, it may have a hard time. In general, it is a good idea for the warm-up period to raise the temperature by a couple of degrees, as this will create better circulation. When the flow of blood through the body increases, the muscles receive more nutrients and are more prepared for the increased needs of the workout. The warm-up period also gives the joints and tendons a chance to limber up before more serious exertion. The movements made during the warm-up period should resemble those that will be made during the core of the work-out, so that the right parts of the body will be prepared.

There are a few different reasons why it is helpful for the body temperature to be increased during the warm-up exercises. For one thing, when the temperature of the muscles is elevated, the metabolic rate of the muscles increases and more oxygen is processed. Also, the nerve impulses are accelerated, making it possible for the fast- and slow-twitch fibers to operate more rapidly. Warmer muscles are more flexible and resilient, which decreases the risk of injury. The production of adenosine triphosphate increases as well, meaning that the muscles have more available energy. All of these factors help eliminate lactic acid from the muscles, thus preventing fatigue and cramps.

CARDIO-RESPIRATORY CONDITIONING

Cardio-respiratory conditioning is simply activity that aims to improve the health of the heart and lungs. Individuals engaging in cardiorespiratory conditioning should gradually increase the intensity of their exertion, to avoid putting a sudden and violent strain on the heart or lungs. There are many different activities that qualify as cardiorespiratory conditioning. Basically, any activity that brings the individual close to his or her target heart rate can be considered cardio-respiratory conditioning. An effective conditioning session will work all of the major muscle groups. Many fitness instructors incorporate music into their cardiorespiratory programs.

COOL-DOWN

The third and final part of a basic work-out is the cool-down period. This is the period in which exertion decreases and the focus is on gradually slowing down in order to preserve flexibility and range of motion. Studies of human physiology have revealed that the cool-down period serves a distinct purpose in a work-out.

MUSCLE CONDITIONING

Every person needs a basic amount of muscle conditioning in order to perform everyday activities. Although muscle conditioning exercises are often associated with bodybuilding in the development of large muscle mass, they actually are a good idea for individuals of all ages and fitness levels. In order to make a muscle conditioning class effective, though, the instructor needs to develop a program that works complementary muscle groups. When large weights are being used, the instructor needs to pay particular attention to proper technique as the risk of injury is elevated. Finally, the instructor should be familiar with the specific fitness goals each participant so that he or she can focus the exercise program on balance, muscular strength, muscular development and flexibility as necessary.

FLEXIBILITY EXERCISES

Every exercise class should include some flexibility exercises, both to increase the range of motion of the joints and to prevent injury. A good stretching routine will be designed to increase the blood flow to the areas of the body that will be used extensively during the body of the workout. Participants should gradually move into every stretching pose without jerking or bouncing. Stretching should not involve pain, but there may be a slight discomfort. As the participants in the exercise class or stretching, the instructor should circulate throughout the room providing pointers on technique and form.

GRADUAL INTENSITY

It is important to gradually increase the intensity of cardiorespiratory exercised so that the heart and lungs can become accustomed to the increased workload. When the body is at rest, the blood tends to concentrate in the internal organs of the trunk, while during exercise the blood is circulated out to the peripheral muscles. The effort required by the heart to make this change is intense. At the same time, the lungs need a warm-up in order to adjust to the increased demand for oxygen in the peripheral muscles. When intense exercise is begun without an adequate warm-up, the result is often hyperventilation or side aches. The best kind of warm-up incorporates the moves that will be used during the main body of the workout. This may involve performing the exact same motions with lower resistance or for performing activities that require a similar motion.

The heart and lungs need time to adjust to the increased workload during exercise. When the body is in a state of rest, the majority of the blood tends to concentrate in the internal organs. When the peripheral muscles begin to work however, more blood is required in the outlying parts of the body, and the heart needs time to meet these demands. At the same time, the respiratory system will need to increase its speed in order to deliver oxygen to the muscles. Otherwise, the elevated circulation of the blood throughout the body will be ineffective because it will not contain enough oxygen. For this reason, exercise programs should begin slowly and only increase in intensity gradually, so that the heart and lungs will have time to adjust to their increased workload.

Exercising too hard, or beginning hard exercise too quickly, can be dangerous. Most people are familiar with the basic signs of over exertion. Dizziness and nausea and hyperventilation are all warning signs of over exertion. Muscle cramps (including the familiar stitch in the side) are indications that the body is not delivering enough oxygen to the muscles. Not only are these conditions dangerous, but they also put the body at risk of further damage. Many studies have confirmed that individuals are at a greater risk of muscle and ligament tears when they are dehydrated or suffering from deficient oxygen. Whenever an individual begins to feel dizzy, or experiences any of the other signs of over exertion, he or she should be encouraged to slowly decrease the intensity of the exercise until the symptoms go away.

In order to provide fitness instruction at the appropriate level of intensity to all the members of the class, the instructor needs to closely monitor the intensity of each participant. Instructor should be aware that most participants in an exercise class will be at a lower level of fitness than the instructor himself. Keeping this in mind, the instructor should slow down to the level of the participants. Participants should always be capable of measuring their own heart rate. Individuals should not be allowed to participate in too many exercise classes in a given week. This is because the body needs sufficient recovery time between high-intensity workouts.

REHEARSAL MOVES

The warm-up moves that directly imitate the moves to be performed in the body of the workout are called rehearsal moves. Whenever possible, the warm-up period of an exercise program should include rehearsal moves, as these are best able to direct blood flow to the right parts of the body. Also performing low intensity or slow rehearsal moves trains the slow twitch and fast twitch muscle fibers for the activity to come. Indeed, many athletes perform rehearsal moves before competition. A fitness instructor should use rehearsal moves when introducing a complex or difficult set of motions. Participants should be encouraged to perform rehearsal moves at their own pace, while the instructor moves about the room providing guidance. The diligent use of rehearsal moves can improve performance and prevent injury.

CHOOSING AND INCORPORATING MOVES

An effective cardiorespiratory program includes all of the muscles that are used in common activities. For instance, it is a good idea to perform exercises that focus on the muscles of the legs that are involved in walking. The cardiorespiratory program should not only work the major muscles of the body but also those muscles that complement the major muscles. When one group of muscles is developed far in advance of another, the potential for injury increases. By developing complementary groups of muscles, balance and flexibility are encouraged.

PROGRESSION AND INTENSITY

In an exercise class, progression is the slow accumulation of moves until a complex exercise sequence has been developed. By beginning with the simplest elements of an activity and gradually increasing the complexity, instructor can maintain the confidence and proper technique of all the participants. Progressing slowly and carefully also helps to reduce the risk of injury. As for intensity, it should always be increased and decreased gradually. This is so that the heart can have a chance to adapt to be increased or decreased demands for blood throughout the body. An effective exercise program will begin with activities that are low intensity.

NECESSARY MODIFICATIONS

In order to maintain the safety of the class during the exercise program, physical fitness instructor needs to be conscious of the three basic indicators of fitness level: age, posture, and knew participant status. Individuals who are extremely young or old will probably not be able to maintain a high-intensity exercise program for a very long time. These individuals should be encouraged to pursue lower intensity exercise than the rest of the class. Individuals with poor posture are likely to be generally out of shape, and may be at greater risk of back injury during certain exercises. Such individuals are also likely to have diminished range of motion. Finally, new participants in an exercise class are likely to be out of shape. Furthermore, individuals who have not participated in exercise classes in the past may need special attention during the teaching of complex maneuvers.

A fitness instructor should always be aware of all the medications that are being taken by the members of the class. For instance, beta-blockers tend to dampen the response of the heart rate to stimulation. In other words, an individual taking this kind of medication will be slow to adjust to the increased demands for oxygen during exercise. Diuretics and large amounts of caffeine will cause an individual to evacuate a great deal of water from the body, thus placing the person at risk of dehydration during exercise. The use of antihistamines, alcohol, cold medicines, diet pills, and tranquilizers can cause lightheadedness and dizziness. Individuals taking these medications should avoid activities that require careful balance or fine motor skills.

Before beginning an exercise class, participants who have serious medical conditions should receive explicit permission from their doctor. Once they have received this permission, however, it is the responsibility of the participants and the fitness instructor to make sure that the fitness program is appropriate and safe. It is a good idea to always err on the side of caution. Individuals who have low functioning heart or lungs should avoid high intensity exercise, and should gradually increase and decrease intensity during the workout. Individuals who suffer diminished function in one of the peripheral joints should avoid activities that place a great deal of strain on the joints in question. Furthermore, such individuals should only perform those activities that are within their comfortable range of motion. At all times, the participants should be monitored closely by the fitness instructor.

As a fitness instructor, you must be attuned to the unique needs of women who are either pregnant or have recently given birth. Such women should only participate in an exercise program with the permission of their doctor. It usually takes about six weeks after giving birth before a woman will be ready to resume exercise. Whether during the pregnant or postpartum period, the intensity of the exercise program should be diminished. Pregnant women are often unsteady on their feet, so any exercise program should avoid difficult balancing. Also, the heart rate and blood pressure can be affected by pregnancy, so these factors should be closely monitored. Finally, pregnant and postpartum women should take special care to stay hydrated during exercise, and to take frequent breaks to restore normal breathing.

Pregnancy causes changes in the body that can adversely affect the ability to exercise. Specifically, the heart is not able to circulate blood through the body as efficiently as before. During exercise, increased demand of blood can inhibit the body's ability to deliver nutrients to the fetus. In particular, pregnant women should avoid lying on their backs for long periods of time. This is because the increased weight in the uterus restricts the blood flow in the blood vessels, particularly the inferior vena cava. In general, pregnant women who are engaging in exercise should have a larger warm up and cool down so the heart and lungs can adapt to the increased demands.

Although it is important for individuals with arthritis to engage in regular exercise, there are special modifications in the exercise program that should be made on their bath. For instance, arthritic joints should not be required to bear heavy loads. This is especially true at the beginning of the exercise class, before the blood flow has increased to the peripheral joints of the body. The primary goal for arthritic participants should be to increase muscle strength around the damaged joints. A certain amount of pain is to be expected, but severe or piercing pain is an indication that the exercise is too intense and should be ceased immediately. Individuals suffering from severe arthritis should only begin an exercise program in consultation with the doctor, and may need to use special braces or straps during the exercise class. Arthritic individuals should avoid the stair climber machine, the elliptical trainer, and any heavy lifting.

A fitness instructor should monitor the performance of senior citizens throughout the exercise program. Any participants who have specific health concerns should participate only to the extent approved by their supervising physician. Senior citizens typically require more warm-up and cool-down time, as their circulation and cardiac function is diminished. Because senior citizens often have poor balance and flexibility, the focus of their exercise should be on gradually improving these components of fitness. An exercise program for senior citizens should avoid high impact and exercises that place excessive weight on a particular area of the body.

Within every exercise class, there will be a few participants who want to either increase or decrease intensity. As an instructor, you need to give students the tools to adjust the level of intensity for themselves. In many cardio-respiratory activities, intensity can be increased simply by speeding up. In flexibility activities, the intensity can be increased by striving for a broader range of motion. In strength exercises, the intensity can be adjusted by manipulating the amount of weight or the number of repetitions performed during each exercise.

A fitness instructor should always be aware of any individuals with disabilities in the exercise class. These individuals are likely to have special needs. For example, individuals with cerebral palsy often have resulting muscle tightness. Individuals with muscular sclerosis will endure a gradual loss of muscle control. Other common disabilities that will require special care in an exercise program are spina bifida and spinal cord injuries. Participants who are suffering from disabilities should bring a physician's evaluation to the beginning of an exercise program. Such individuals should not be required to participate in any activities that have an increased likelihood of injury, or require exceptional balance. During the class, the instructor should be extremely attentive to the needs of all disabled participants.

Fitness instructors need to take special care regarding all participants who suffer from coronary heart disease. Any individual suffering from coronary heart disease must have the approval of his or her physician before beginning an exercise program. Such individuals will need an extended warm-up time. During the warm-up, individuals with coronary heart disease should pay special attention to their physical signs, making sure that dizziness or chest discomfort does not develop. The instructor should always ask such participants if they've taken their medication. Indeed, a fitness instructor should have a detailed list of all the medications the participant is taking regularly. Individuals with coronary heart disease should check their heart rate often, and should use more specific techniques for doing so.

Respiratory disorders can prevent the lungs from delivering the necessary oxygen to the muscle cells during exercise. For this reason, any participants in an exercise class who suffer from asthma, emphysema, or chronic bronchitis should be monitored closely. Before the initiation of an exercise program, individuals with respiratory disorders should inform the instructor as to any medications or special requirements. Moreover, the participants should have conferred with their doctor before beginning such a program. During a fitness class, individuals with respiratory disorders can use a peak flow meter, in order to monitor their respiratory condition. If breathing becomes difficult or there is pain in the chest, the individual should stop exercising immediately. Individuals who suffer from respiratory disorders should have a longer warm up and cool down time. Intensity should always be increased and decreased gradually.

ENVIRONMENTAL FACTORS

Fitness instructors should take special care in the arrangement of participants during exercise class. The most common arrangement is to have the participants standing or sitting in rows. This is perhaps the most effective way to fit a large number of students into a small area, but it may prevent the instructor from seeing participants in the back of the classroom. This is especially problematic when the most experienced and fit members of the class cluster towards the front, near the instructor. If this becomes a problem, the instructor should take special care to circulate throughout the room during the exercise class. If possible, the instructor may want to put the members of the class in a circle or semicircle. One thing wrong with these arrangements, however, is that they force the members of the class to look directly at one another. Self-conscious members of an exercise class may be uncomfortable with this arrangement.

An ideal exercise facility should be well ventilated and neither too hot nor too cold. Most experts agree that the appropriate temperature for an exercise class is around 70° Fahrenheit. The floor of the exercise facility should be springy enough to cushion the impact of intense exercise, but not so bouncy that it will diminish the balance of the participants. Many exercise classes are equipped with mirrors on all the walls, so that the participants can monitor their own performance during the class. It may be helpful for the instructor to stand on a dais, or raised platform, so that he or she can be seen by all the participants in the class. Finally, it is essential that the participants in the class have access to water at all times; many exercise facilities have water fountains within the room.

Part of the job of a fitness instructor is to ensure that the classroom environment contributes to the success of students. The physical environment should be bright, clean, and safe, so that participants will feel optimistic and secure while participating in the program. Any music chosen for a class should be upbeat and inoffensive, to avoid alienating any participants who might be intimidated by the requirements of the class. Finally, one of the most crucial elements of the classroom environment is the rapport that you build with your students. By using positive language, eye contact, and a smile, you can vastly improve your students' chances of adhering to a long-term fitness program.

The participants in an exercise class are more likely to be successful when the classroom environment is friendly and efficient. The instructor should greet each of the students by name as they enter the class. If there are new students, the instructor should take the time to learn their names and a little bit about their fitness goals. Once the class begins, the instructor should give students positive reinforcement and gentle correction. The instructor should be familiar with each participant's level of fitness; so as to make sure that the work-out is beneficial for individuals at all levels.

HEALTH SCREEN DOCUMENT

The basic health screen document is a series of questions regarding individual medical and fitness history. A fitness instructor should have every member of a fitness class fell out of health screen document at the initiation of the exercise program. A health screen document should include the individual's history of exercise, eating habits, recent illnesses, history of illness, fitness goals, and any other pertinent information. If the information given on the health screen document indicates any serious medical problems, the participant should receive explicit permission from his or her doctor before beginning the exercise program. A fitness instructor should carefully study the health screen document, as it will contain information that will allow him or her to best meet the needs of each participant in the class.

EMERGENCY CONTACT

If a medical emergency develops during a fitness class, the emergency services should be contacted immediately. Until trained medical personnel can arrive, the instructor should stay with the victim. The fitness instructor should always have access to a telephone, and should know the appropriate numbers to call for emergency care. The fitness instructor should also be able to provide detailed driving directions to the emergency services.

FITNESS ASSESSMENT

There are a few different reasons why it is important to incorporate fitness assessments into exercise classes. For one thing, they allow the instructor to gauge each participant's basic level of fitness, so that the exercise program can be tailored to his or her needs. Fitness assessments also give people a way to measure the changes in their level of fitness; this can be very encouraging for people who wonder whether their hard work is having any effect. The exact fitness assessments that are used will depend on the area of fitness to be measured: there are basic tests for flexibility, strength, and cardiovascular endurance that can easily be taught to the participants in an exercise class.

There are a couple of quick ways to measure fitness. In a body mass index test, the amount of fat mass in the body is compared to the amount of muscle mass. The body mass index can be quickly derived by dividing weight in kilograms by the square of the height in meters. Women with a BMI over 27.3%, and men with a BMI over 27.8%, are considered overweight, while anyone with a BMI over 30% is considered obese. In the waist-to-hip circumference measure, a tape measure is used to find the ratio of the circumference of the waist at its smallest point to the hips at their broadest point.

The step test and push-up/half sit-up tests are used to gauge an individual's cardiovascular and muscular strength, respectively. In the step test, the individual steps on and off of a small platform at a moderate rate for three minutes, at which point his or her heart rate should be measured. In the push-up test, the individual should do as many full push-ups as possible, resting only in the "up" position. This test lasts until the muscles are incapable of performing another push-up. The half sit-up test is similar, except that instead of doing push-ups the individual lies supine with his or her hands and feet flat on the floor, and then flexes his or her abdominal muscles until his or her hands have moved approximately 3 and a half inches.

In a shoulder flexibility test, the individual puts one arm straight up in the air, and then bends his elbow so that his hand falls in between his shoulder blades. The individual then reaches behind his back with the other hand, and the distance between the two hands is the test score.

TARGET HEART RATE

There are a few different ways to determine an individual's target heart rate. One of these ways is called the "percentage of maximal heart rate" method. An individual's maximal heart rate is calculated by subtracting the individual's age from 220. Note that this is not a precise means of determining maximal heart rate, so individuals with heart conditions should always seek further information. Using this basic formula, however, the target heart rate can then be found by multiplying maximal heart rate, the percent of intensity desired, and 1.15. For instance, then, a 20-year-old individual seeking to exercise at 60% intensity would have a target heart rate of 138.

One of the common methods of determining the target heart rate is known as the "percent of heart rate reserve," or Karvonen, method. This method requires both the maximal heart rate (age in years subtracted from 220) and the resting heart rate. The resting heart rate is subtracted from the maximal heart rate, the target percentage of maximal heart rate is taken from it, and the resting heart rate is added to this number. As an example, consider a 20-year-old individual with a resting heart rate of 80 who wishes to exercise at 75% intensity. Resting heart rate subtracted from maximal heart rate will be 120, and 75% of 120 is 90. The resting heart rate of 80 is then added, setting the target heart rate at 170.

Another common method of gauging target heart rate is the "rate of perceived exertion" method. This method does not rely on any actual measurements, such as maximal or resting heart rate. To determine target heart rate using the rate of perceived exertion, the individual gauges his or her level of exertion on a scale (either 1-10 or 6-20). In order to facilitate this self-assessment, most rates of perceived exertion scales will have lists of common activities, so that the individual knows walking is a certain rate of exertion, while sprinting is another.

Individuals who suffer from chronic lung conditions like asthma or emphysema may be best served by the "dyspnea scale" method of determining target heart rate. In this method, the ability to breathe is placed on a scale of 0 to 4. Breathing easily and slowly is a 0. Breathing that is slightly more difficult but not discernibly different to an outside observer is classified as a 1. Breathing that is labored enough to be noticed by an outside observer is classified as a 2. Breathing that is more difficult, but not so difficult that exercise is impossible, is classified as a 3. Finally, breathing that is so laborious that exercise is impossible is classified as a 4. Individuals should decrease the intensity of exercise any time they reach 3 on the dyspnea scale.

The "talk test" method is one of the simplest ways to determine target heart rate. If an individual has no difficulty talking, then the intensity of the exercise is not too great. If carrying on a conversation becomes a bit more laborious, the intensity of the exercise can be classified as moderate. When conversation is only possible while gasping for breath, the exercise is too intense and should be decreased. Obviously, the talk test is not a very exact means of measuring target heart rate, and is much more effective for beginning exercisers.

CHECKING HEART RATE

It is important for all people, and particularly for beginning exercisers, to constantly monitor heart rate during a work-out. The heart rate should always be ascertained at the peripheral rather than the carotid artery, and the individual should continue moving while checking his or her pulse. This prevents the blood from concentrating in the lower extremities and preventing an accurate assessment of the heart rate. The heart rate should be calculated using a ten-second pulse count; any music or verbal cues that have the potential to interfere with accurate counting should be suspended for the duration of the pulse count.

MEASURING CARDIORESPIRATORY ENDURANCE

In order to exercise at or near the target heart rate for a long period of time, an individual needs to have lungs that are capable of distributing oxygen to the muscles rapidly and efficiently. This capacity is known as cardiorespiratory endurance. There are a number of ways to measure cardiorespiratory endurance, including the 12-minute walk and run test, the Rockport walking test, and a very precise test that measures the volume of oxygen in the blood during exercise. Before initiating an exercise program, individuals should acquire a basic understanding of their own cardiorespiratory endurance.

MEASURING BODY COMPOSITION

There are a few common ways to measure body composition. In the method known as bioelectrical impedance, tiny electrical impulses are sent through the body tissue. Because lean body tissue conducts electricity more quickly than fatty tissue, the system is able to generate a fairly reliable assessment of body composition. Anthropometric assessment is the technical term given to any direct measurement of the body, as for instance with calipers or tape measure. Hydrostatic weighing is an assessment of the density of the body that is conducted by submerging the individual in a tub of water. Lean tissue has a different density than fatty tissue, so the relative buoyancy of the individual can be used to determine body composition.

INSTRUCTOR'S ATTIRE

The instructor's choice of attire should be designed to create the most positive atmosphere for all the members of the class. The instructor's clothing should be chosen with the decorum and function in mind. For instance, instructors who are leading a swimming class should be wearing swim trunks. Swimwear, however, should not be too revealing. Indeed, instructors should always select clothing that does not have the potential to intimidate participants who may feel insecure about their own appearance. Before the initiation of an exercise program, instructor should provide information to all participants about appropriate clothing, and the instructor should follow these requirements as well.

PREPARING FOR CLASS

The most important thing a fitness instructor can do before the beginning of an exercise program is to acquire all relevant information about the participants' health histories and physical needs. This is especially important when some participants have health problems that may inhibit their participation in the class, or may increase their risk of injury. The instructor should provide information as to the intensity of the class, as well as the intensity that will be reached during each class. The instructor should also discuss appropriate attire for the class, as well as the class format. Finally, the instructor should inform participants as to whether they will need to bring any special equipment to class, and should encourage participants to bring water to each class.

Different fitness classes will often have wildly different objectives and needs, depending on the experience and fitness level of the members of the class. A fitness instructor needs to be sensitive to the differences between classes, and able to make adjustments that will enable each class to reach their overall objectives. In some classes, for instance, it will be necessary to place special emphasis on flexibility. In other classes, cardiorespiratory endurance will be the component of fitness that requires the most attention. At all times, the instructor should remain flexible and willing to make any changes that could improve the effectiveness of the exercise program. Although it is important to develop a loose structure for each class beforehand, it is also essential to be able to make necessary adjustments in real time.

CHOICE OF EQUIPMENT

Fitness instructors should always inform participants in each exercise class as to the equipment that will be required for the class. Any equipment to be used in a physical fitness class should be checked and maintained for safety by the instructor. Some of the more common types of equipment used in physical fitness classes are resistance tools, such as bands and small weights, and cardiorespiratory equipment, as, for instance, steps. Unless the class is being administered at advanced level, the instructor is responsible for making sure that all participants know how to use the equipment.

Before developing a fitness program, the instructor should take into account the quality of the floor in the fitness room. The floor of the exercise room needs to be sufficiently springy to absorb shocks of running and jumping. Also, the floor needs to provide enough traction so that the participants in the class can move around without being at risk of slipping and falling. Hardwood floors are good for exercising, as long as there is sufficient padding underneath. Some carpets are appropriate for exercise classes, as long as the fringe is not too long. Exercise classes may be conducted outdoors, as long as the grass is not too long and the surface is not too uneven.

In order to be effective, physical fitness equipment must be used according to certain basic rules. A fitness instructor should regularly check equipment for signs of wear and tear. Fitness equipment should only be used for the purpose for which it was designed. Before beginning a section of the fitness class in which the equipment is to be used, the instructor should make sure that all the participants are familiar with its operation. As participants in the class begin to use the fitness equipment, the instructor should circulate throughout the room and monitor the participants to make sure that safety guidelines are being followed.

Before the initiation of an exercise program, the instructor should make sure that all the appropriate equipment is available. Floor exercises will require some kind of mat, while strength enhancement exercises will probably involve some kind of resistance training equipment. Other common needs during aerobic classes are jump ropes, steps, and Swedish balls. The instructor should know how to use all the necessary equipment for the class. Finally, if the instructor wants to play music during the class, he or she should make sure that a stereo system is present.

RELAXATION AND VISUALIZATION

Many fitness instructors use the beginning and end of an exercise class to promote relaxation and motivation by leading the participants in some visualization exercises. Many instructors find that the class will have more success if they take a few minutes to decompress before beginning. During this time, an instructor may choose to play quiet music or simply to have the room in silence. The instructor can describe specific calming images to the class, or may ask the class to visualize any thoughts or ideas that are especially calming to them. During this period, the participants should also be breathing deeply and making a point of relaxing all of their muscles.

USE OF MUSIC

Many fitness instructors use music to good effect in their fitness classes. The choice of music, however, will depend on the character of the fitness class. Aerobic classes will benefit from up-tempo music that participants can follow. During periods of relaxation, slower music will encourage participants to relax and concentrate on their bodies. It is important that music not be so loud that the instructor's verbal cues cannot be heard. In some classes, an instructor may want to include music that the participants can sing along with, as the ability to maintain singing is an indication that participants are not working at too great an intensity.

The music played during an exercise class can also affect the safety of the class if it is too loud. Most obviously, music that is played at an extremely high decibel level can be damaging to the ears. In an exercise class, the participants are also at greater risk of injury if they cannot hear the instructions of the teacher. Music that is so loud that the participants cannot hear the verbal cues of the instructor can be considered dangerous. Such volume levels can also be dangerous for the instructor, if he or she has to strain his or her voice in order to be heard.

For a fitness instructor, the most important thing about the music used in an exercise class is the tempo. Tempo is typically measured in beats per minute. A tempo under 100 beats per minute is considered to be fairly slow, and is therefore appropriate for the warm-up and cool down periods, especially while stretching. Slightly faster tempos are appropriate for the warm-up and cool down times as well, especially when the class is engaging in low impact, low intensity cardiorespiratory exercise. Faster aerobic exercise is best performed to music with a tempo between 120 and 150 beats per minute. During aerobic exercise, a fitness instructor should be conscious of the musical measures. For instance, it is best to initiate a new exercise maneuver on the first beat of the measure. All of the major steps in a complicated maneuver should be performed either on the beats or on the half beat of each measure.

PROMOTING SELF-RESPONSIBILITY

Even a student-centered fitness instructor is unable to monitor every member of the class at the same time. For this reason, the instructor should always strive to cultivate self-responsibility in all of the class participants. Specifically, every participant in an exercise program should learn to monitor their own level of intensity and heart rate. Each participant should be aware when his or her level of intensity is too high. Developing responsibility among the participants in an exercise class means teaching them the balance between following the instructor and paying attention to their own needs. It will take time to develop the skill in all the participants in the class, but an instructor can speed the process by providing constant verbal cues and encouraging participants when necessary.

MONITORING HEART RATE

Every member of a fitness class should be able to measure his or her own heart rate. The two most common sites for measuring the heart rate are the carotid artery and the radial artery. The carotid artery is found on the right side of the neck. In order to check the pulse there, one should be lightly press two fingers to the artery. The radial artery, meanwhile, is found at the wrist. It too should be measured with light pressure from two fingers. When students are first learning to take their own heart rate, they may want to count the beats for a full minute. In time, though, students should be able to extrapolate the heart rate after only counting the pulses for 10 seconds.

LEARNING MOTOR SKILLS

An individual who learns a motor skill passes through three distinct stages: the cognitive stage, the associative stage, and the autonomous stage. In the cognitive stage, the participants will not have fully understood the steps in the skill. He or she will have to make an effort to remember the steps, and therefore will not be able to perform the skill fluidly. In the associative stage, the participants will remember the steps of the skill, and will be concentrating on refining it. In the autonomous stage of learning, the individual will be able to perform the skill without receiving any external assistance. At this point, the individual will be able to perform the activity without having to consciously remember the steps.

PROGRAM GOALS

A fitness instructor sets goals in order to define the purpose of a fitness program and to develop fitness knowledge in the class participants. Many studies have shown that exercise program participants have a higher rate of success when they have clear goals to work towards. The goals for a fitness program may be very specific or very general. For instance, some class participants may aspire to a specific level of muscular strength, muscular endurance, or flexibility. These would be examples of specific goals. On the other hand, participants may simply seek to have improved energy or better perceived quality of life. These would be examples of general goals.

When setting the goals and expectations for a fitness class, the instructor needs to take care that they are realistic. If the expectations of the instructor are set too high, it is likely that the participants in the class will become discouraged with their own performance. The instructor must walk a fine line between setting expectations too low, and thus failing to challenge students, and setting expectations too high, and thus discouraging them. A fitness instructor should work with the participants in the class to formulate realistic goals before the exercise program is initiated. When necessary, a fitness instructor should be able to gently indicate to students that some goals are unrealistic in the short-term.

Creating a systematic class design means organizing every exercise class to best benefit the particular participants in it. The fitness instructor should always have specific goals and objectives for each fitness class. These goals should be made clear to all the participants at the beginning of the class, and a fitness instructor should outline the specific steps that will be taken to meet these goals. At the end of each class, the instructor should inform the participants as to whether the class has been successful in working towards the goals, and what steps may need to be taken in order to improve performance in the future. If possible, the instructor should develop personalized exercise programs for each of the participants in the class.

Many fitness instructors make the mistake of trying to plan their exercise programs on the fly. By planning ahead, the instructor will be more likely to select activities that efficiently lead the class towards the exercise goals. Indeed, the beginning point of the planning process should be the fitness objectives of the class. For instance, if a class has set as a goal the improvement of flexibility, the instructor will want to select activities that are geared towards this goal. If the goal of the class is to improve cardiorespiratory endurance, the instructor may want to extend the period of high intensity aerobic exercise, possibly by diminishing the duration of muscular strength exercises.

COMMAND STYLE OF INSTRUCTION

One of the common kinds of instruction used in fitness classes is known as the command style. In the command style of instruction, the instructor makes all decisions about exercise program. The participants in the class have no input into the content or pace of the class. One of the problems with the command style is that it is very difficult to adjust the intensity according to the particular needs of individuals within the class. Teachers who use the command style are likely to find that individuals at the extremes of a fitness range are not satisfied. One advantage of the command style of instruction is that it allows the instructor to maintain control over the class and monitor safety issues closely.

Fitness instructors can be divided into two categories: teacher-centered instructors and student-centered instructors. Teacher-centered instructors perform the class exercises at the same time as the participants without circulating through the class and providing verbal cues. Student-centered instructors, meanwhile, do not continuously perform class exercises, but instead circulate throughout the class and provide guidance. In general, the participants in a fitness program succeed more with student-centered instructors. This is mainly because they feel more involved in the class and are able to receive more personal treatment from the instructor.

EXECUTION OF EXERCISES

Throughout an exercise class, a fitness instructor should take special care to make sure that participants are performing all exercises with proper technique. This is especially important during those exercises which may result in injury if performed incorrectly. In many exercises, the back must be kept perfectly straight to avoid undue strain. Furthermore, many back exercises can perpetuate poor posture if they are performed incorrectly. Any exercises that have the potential for damage should be taught at a low intensity first.

In order to keep an exercise class safe and effective, an instructor needs to teach in small concise steps. In other words, the participants in the class should not be told to perform a complex series of movements before they have fully understood the process. In addition, the intensity level of the exercise should be kept at a moderate level until participants have fully learned for sequence. The instructor should be careful to circulate throughout the room monitoring the performance of all the participants in the class. Special attention should be paid to the posture and spinal alignment of each participant, as errors in posture can often lead to serious back injury.

ACCOMMODATING VARIOUS LEVELS

No matter how specific the theme of an exercise class, a fitness instructor will have to deal with participants of varying fitness levels. Learning to provide adequate instruction to a broad spectrum of abilities is one of the main challenges confronting a beginning fitness instructor. One way to ensure that individuals exercise with the proper intensity is to make sure that they frequently monitor their own heart rate. This way, each participant in the exercise class can adjust the intensity of his or her activity in order to stay within the target heart rate zone. The instructor should always be available to help individuals make these adjustments. As for the music in the exercise class, it should always be at a tempo appropriate for the least fit members of the class.

STRAINS

Strains, otherwise known as polled muscles, manifest themselves in pain, diminished range of motion, and diminished strength. Oftentimes, a muscle strain will not be accompanied by any visible symptoms; in some cases, however, there may be swelling or discoloration. The best immediate treatment for a muscle strain is rest and ice. If possible, the affected muscle should be stretched. Under no circumstances should a strained muscle be subjected to high-intensity or severe stretching. After a muscle has been strained, it should not be used fully until the signs of strain are reduced.

TENDONITIS

Tendonitis is a common condition in which a tendon becomes inflamed. Tendons are the durable fibers that connect muscles to bones in the body. Repetitive or violent stress on a tendon can lead to tendonitis, which typically manifests as pain and decreased range of motion. Tendonitis is especially common in middle-aged and elderly individuals. The most common areas where tendonitis develops are the hands, the upper arms near the shoulder, and in the ankle (Achilles tendon). There is no immediate cure for tendonitis; the typical recommendation is simply rest of the afflicted area.

ANKLE SPRAIN

The lateral ankle sprain is one of the more common injuries associated with exercise and athletic competition. They are especially common among older individuals in whom the muscles surrounding the ankle may be weaker. An ankle sprain is simply a strain or severing of the ligaments on either side of the ankle. When it occurs, the individual will typically experience a brief flash of pain and a popping noise. The ankle will swell up for several days after a sprain. There is no immediate treatment for a lateral ankle sprain; most doctors will recommend the treatment plan known by the acronym RICE: rest, ice, compression, and elevation.

A sprain is a painful wrenching or laceration of the tendons or ligaments surrounding a joint. These injuries occur most often in the ankles, knees, and wrists. If the tendon or ligament is subjected to repeated or violent stress, it will typically become inflamed. When this occurs, the individual will experience pain and decreased range of motion. There is often some swelling in the area, as the body directs blood to the afflicted area to aid in the healing process.

PLANTAR FASCIITIS

Plantar fasciitis is a condition in which the connective tissue that supports the arch of the foot becomes inflamed. Individuals suffering from plantar fasciitis will typically experience pain on the bottom of the heel, especially during the first few steps of the day. This condition is associated with obesity, sudden weight gain, excessive exercise, and wearing shoes with insufficient arch support. There is no immediate cure for plantar fasciitis, though the condition has a positive long-term prognosis. Usually rest will be enough to alleviate the symptoms of the condition, though aspirin and ibuprofen may also be useful.

ROTATOR CUFF

Rotator cuff strain is a common injury. The four muscles of the shoulder (supraspinatus, infraspinatus, teres minor, and subscapularis) are connected to the scapula, humerus, and clavicles through a network of tendons. These tendons are likely to become inflamed during activities that involve repetitive or violent stress to the shoulder, like swimming, tennis, and baseball. All of these activities require the raising of the arm above the head. This kind of injury becomes especially common in middle age, as the blood flow to this area decreases. For minor strains, rest is typically a sufficient treatment

When a rotator cuff is impinged, the rotator cuff tendon has become pinched. This typically happens when the rotator cuff has been called upon to do strenuous work, especially when the arms have been extended over the head for a long period of time. Although some impingement of the rotator cuff may require surgery or anti-inflammatory injections, most can be treated with rest and ice. Individuals who experience any pain in the rotator cuff should cease exercises that involve raising the arms above the head. Exercises that place a great deal of strain on the rotator cuff, as for instance pull ups and the military press, should be avoided as well.

ANTERIOR SHOULDER

Anterior shoulder instability usually occurs in one of two forms: dislocation and subluxation. In a shoulder dislocation, the rounded end of the humerus is not entirely out of its socket. A shoulder dislocation is extremely painful, and each successive dislocation makes it more likely that further dislocations will occur in the future. Describing a shoulder dislocation as anterior means that the ball of the humerus has popped out of the front of the joint. A subluxation, meanwhile, occurs when the humerus briefly is forced out of its socket, but immediately returns. Some individuals are especially disposed to subluxation, and can endure shoulder instability with little pain. For others, even the briefest subluxation is extremely painful and results in swelling and diminished range of motion.

LATERAL EPICONDYLITIS

Lateral epicondylitis, more commonly known as tennis elbow, is a common condition caused by repetitive or violent stress placed on the tendons of the elbow joint. This condition gets its informal name because it is associated with sports that require repetitive flexing of the forearm and wrist muscles. An individual suffering from lateral epicondylitis will typically experience pain or tenderness in the elbow, and may lose some grip strength.

ANTERIOR CRUCIATE LIGAMENT

One of the more common but serious injuries suffered during non-contact athletic competition is the tearing of the anterior cruciate ligament. This often occurs when an individual rapidly decelerates or changes direction. For this reason, torn ACLs are most common in basketball, soccer, and football. This injury is quite painful, and will usually prevent the individual from walking. If the ACL is only partially torn, it may be allowed to heal on its own; more severe cases will require surgery.

SHIN SPLINTS

Many frequent runners and other athletes suffer chronic pain along the tibia, otherwise known as shin splints. This pain is caused by an excessive amount of pressure over a long period of time on the shin bone (tibia) and its connective tissues. Shin splints typically manifests with tenderness and pain on the inner part of the leg below the knee. This pain may be accompanied by mild swelling. If exercise is not ceased, over time this pain may be present even while resting. The best treatment for shin splints is rest and ice. In order to prevent Shin splints before they occur, athletes should avoid running on hard surfaces for long distances, and should frequently purchase new athletic shoes.

PATELLOFEMORAL PAIN DISORDERS

Patellofemoral pain disorder, otherwise known as runner's knee, is a condition in which the kneecap comes into contact with the end of the femur when the knee is flexed. Patellofemoral pain disorder typically occurs because of excessive use. For minor cases of runner's knee, rest and ice are sufficient. In more severe cases, however, surgery may be necessary. In order to provide extra support to the knee, one may elect to use tapes or braces. While recuperating from patellofemoral pain disorder, individuals should avoid extreme bending of the knee, as for instance in a full squat.

LOWER BACK PAIN

Many individuals suffer from chronic low back pain. This period can be the result of genetic factors, injuries, or abnormalities of the spine. Individuals suffering from chronic low back pain will likely have a diminished range of motion and strength, and may suffer debilitating pains during exercise. A fitness instructor should always be aware of those members of the class who suffer from chronic low back pain. The instructor should take special care to ensure that these participants keep their backs straight during intense exercise, as poor posture can exacerbate an already existing back problem. The warm-up period for individuals with low back pain should always include long, slow stretches of the lower back.

PROPER FOOTWEAR

Just as proper flooring is important in an exercise class, so is proper footwear. Many aerobic and cardiorespiratory activities involve significant impact on the feet, and so the health of the joints needs to be protected with adequate footwear. Classes such as kickboxing and step require shoes with ample support for the front of the foot, as these activities require bouncing on the balls of the feet. Other aerobic classes in which there is a great deal of lateral movement require shoes that provide special ankle support, to prevent the ankle from rolling over during slide maneuvers.

EMERGENCY PLAN

Every exercise facility must have a detailed emergency plan. Every instructor and staff member at the facility must be familiar with the emergency plan and it must be reviewed and updated regularly. At least once every year the employees of the facility should practice what to do in case of an emergency. Also, the facility should be stocked with all documentation that will be necessary in the event of an emergency. Finally, the participants in an exercise class should provide contact information so that their friends and relatives may be contacted in the event of an emergency.

If an emergency arises during an exercise class, the instructor should immediately attend to it. Another member of the class should call emergency services while the instructor attends to the injured participant. Fitness instructors should always be

skilled in first aid and cardiopulmonary resuscitation. Also, the fitness instructor should be aware of any pre-existing medical conditions. The fitness instructor should stay with the victim until the arrival of the emergency services, providing whatever care is appropriate. Documentation of the emergency should not be completed until emergency services have arrived.

FIRST AID KIT

Every exercise facility needs to have a well-stocked and up-to-date first-aid kit. Every instructor and staff member should know its location. A complete first-aid kit should include bandages, gauze, elastic wraps, antibacterial soap, antibiotic cream, a blood pressure cuff, stethoscope, scissors, ice packs, latex gloves, a paper bag, and splinting material. Whenever an emergency arises in which blood and bodily fluid are present, latex gloves should be used by all attending employees. Also, any equipment or space in the exercise facility that comes into contact with blood or bodily fluid should be cleaned thoroughly with liquid soap and an admixture of bleach and water.

Exercise Science

FITNESS COMPONENTS

The five components of physical fitness are muscular strength, muscular endurance, cardiovascular endurance, flexibility, and body composition. Every person has some degree of muscular strength. This is the greatest amount of force that a muscle or group of muscles is able to exert. Muscular endurance, meanwhile, is the ability of the muscle or muscle groups to work for a long duration. Measures of muscular endurance typically involve performing a relatively easy action a large number of times. Cardiovascular endurance is the measure of the lungs, heart, and blood vessels to provide oxygen and other nutrients to the muscles and tissues as well as to get rid of toxic wastes that build up in the muscles. Flexibility is the measure of the body's range of motion. Finally, body composition is the ratio of lean body mass to body fat.

ATP

Adenosine triphosphate (ATP) is the chemical required for proper muscle function. ATP is responsible for metabolism, muscle contraction, and the ability of the cell to synthesize proteins. ATP is derived from food. When a person eats something, part of the food is converted into ATP. Some of this ATP is used to repair tissue, while other ATP is turned into glycogen or stored as fat. These are the chemical components that make exercise possible. Specifically, ATP enables enzyme metabolism and muscle contraction.

The ATP derived from food is not always put to immediate use. Some of it is stored for future use. When it is required by cells, it can be re-synthesized with the help of the organic compound creatine phosphate. Specifically, ATP is stored as adenosine diphosphate, until it combines with phosphocreatine during intense muscle contraction. This process can be reversed, making it possible for muscles to respond to fluctuating demands. The body can thus prevent excess levels of ATP from building up in the muscles.

ANAEROBIC GLYCOLYSIS

Anaerobic glycolysis is the process through which sugars can be broken down into lactic acid, ethanol, and the chemical adenosine triphosphate. In anaerobic glycolysis, this process is accomplished without oxygen. Anaerobic glycolysis is able to create muscle energy with a longer duration than the ATP-CP system. The downside of anaerobic glycolysis is that it also generates pyruvic acid. Pyruvic acid, like lactic acid, can cause cramping and fatigue if it is allowed to linger in the muscle tissue. The steady flow of oxygen through the muscle cells encourages the removal of these acids.

AEROBIC PRODUCTION OF ATP

In order to perform high intensity work, the muscles must produce their own adenosine triphosphate. Aerobic glycolysis is the process, also known as cellular respiration, in which sugars are converted into adenosine triphosphate using oxygen. Aerobic glycolysis is responsible for most of the creation of energy within a cell. During this process, the cells produce carbon dioxide, which will then be transported back to the lungs and expelled from the body. Aerobic glycolysis helps evacuate toxins and acids from the muscles, thus preventing fatigue and cramping.

FATTY ACID OXIDATION

Much of the energy produced by the body is created during the process known as fatty acid oxidation. This process is also known as beta oxidation. Fatty acids are typically found in animal and vegetable fats and oils. They may be either saturated or unsaturated. Some fatty acids, known as triglycerides, are capable of providing two times as much energy as carbohydrates or proteins. The metabolism of a fatty acid is either a catabolic or anabolic process. In catabolic metabolism, fatty acids are broken down into smaller units. In anabolic metabolism, fatty acids are synthesized into the tissues of the human body.

ENERGY TERMINOLOGY

A kilocalorie is the amount of energy required to raise the temperature of 1 kg of water by 1°C. Caloric expenditure is a complex measurement of the amount of calories burned by the human body. The sum total of calories consumed by the body is referred to as the caloric intake. The caloric deficit is the number of calories that must be burned in order for a person to lose weight. The individual must burn more calories than he or she consumes in order to lose weight. The condition of equilibrium in which one consumes the same amount of calories as one burns is known as energy balance.

CARBOHYDRATES

In order to create ATP, the body needs a healthy supply of sugars. This supply mainly comes from the consumption of carbohydrates. The carbohydrates that are consumed in food and drinks are broken down by the body into the sugar glucose.

Carbohydrates may be either simple or complex. Simple carbohydrates come from nature, as for instance fruit and honey. Simple carbohydrates may also come from refined sugars. Complex carbohydrates, on the other hand, contain more vitamins, minerals, and nutrients.

PROTEINS

In order to function properly, a human being must ingest a certain amount of protein. The protein is a complex organic molecule that contains oxygen, nitrogen, hydrogen, and carbon. Proteins are necessary for the formation and maintenance of body tissue. For human beings, the primary sources of proteins are meat, fish, milk, eggs, and nuts. Proteins are essential for the creation of DNA. The bones of the human body are composed of approximately one quarter proteins and in the organs and fluids of the body also contain protein in large part. Proteins also play an important role in neurological function. Many studies have shown that Alzheimer's disease, to name just one, is the result of deficient proteins in the brain.

FATS

Fats, otherwise known as lipids, can be divided into a few different categories. Saturated fatty acids are solid at room temperature and are associated with heart disease. Monounsaturated fatty acids, on the other hand, are healthy. Polyunsaturated fatty acids are useful in blood clotting, and are found in fish and plant oils. Triglycerides are commonly found in vegetable and animal fats and oils. The human body uses fat for a number of purposes. Fat provides insulation and protection for the internal organs. It also is readily broken down and converted into energy.

GOLGI TENDONS AND SPINDLES

Golgi tendon organs are fibers made up of collagen that connect the body of a tendon to muscle fibers. When the muscle is contracted, the Golgi tendon organ is stretched. It then relays information about muscle strength to the brain. This information is used in the performance of future muscle contractions. A muscle spindle, meanwhile, is a long fiber contained within the meat of the muscle. Muscle spindles are stimulated whenever the muscle is lengthened or shortened. They send information about the function of the muscle to the central nervous system.

FACTORS EFFECTING MOVEMENT

The complex coordinated movements of the human body require a number of conscious and unconscious processes. For instance, the brain and nervous system must collect and process data concerning the contractions of the muscles and the quality of the objects in the external environment. The proprioceptive sense is the body's unconscious perception of its own movement as well as its position within the physical world. The kinesthetic sense, meanwhile, is the body's ability to note and take account of the movements of its various parts. In order to coordinate movements, the body needs to be able to accurately assess its own position as well as the quality and position of the objects outside of the body.

EXERCISE SPECIFICITY

When an individual performs exercises that are designed to work certain muscles, he or she is practicing exercise specificity. Exercise specificity is essential for reaching specific fitness goals. For example, it would be silly for an individual seeking to improve her cardiovascular fitness to focus entirely on resistance training. Instead, she would be best served by prolonged cardiorespiratory exercise at moderate intensity. Similarly, a sprinter would not be well served by a running program that only includes long distance runs. In order to increase explosive speed and train the fast twitch muscle fibers of the legs, a sprinter needs to train by performing short, high intensity runs.

MUSCLE FIBERS

The muscles of the human body have two basic types of fibers. Slow twitch fibers are more efficient in their use of oxygen, and typically get their energy from aerobic glycolysis. The slow twitch fibers are more integral in the performance of long term, low intensity exercise. Fast twitch fibers, on the other hand, are able to generate energy quickly, through anaerobic glycolysis. The fast twitch fibers are utilized for quick, violent movements. Many of the muscles in the human body contain both slow twitch and fast twitch fibers.

STANDING STRETCHES

Most exercise classes contain some basic flexibility exercises at either the beginning or the end. There are four basic stretches that are performed from a standing position. The hamstring stretch, the individual extends one leg in front of the other and leans forward, such that the extended leg is bent. The gastronomies muscle can be stretched in this same position, by leaning forward over the front foot. By then leaning backward and bending the back knee, the soleus is stretched. In this position, the shoulder extensors can be stretched by reaching up and back with the hands pressed together.

MUSCULAR CONTRACTIONS

Muscle contractions may be isometric, isokinetic, or isotonic. In an isometric muscle contraction, the muscle does not decrease or increase in length. This kind of contraction occurs when pushing or pulling on a stationary object. Isokinetic contractions, meanwhile, either shorten or lengthen the muscle. Furthermore, the muscle remains in a state of tension throughout its extension or truncation. In an isotonic contraction, finally, the muscle is either lengthened or shortened. In an isotonic contraction, the muscle is under its greatest tension at its greatest length.

VALSALVA MANEUVER

The Valsalva maneuver is performed by forcing air out of the lungs with the mouth and nostrils forcibly closed. This process drives the air into the Eustachian tubes, and places a great deal of pressure on the eardrum. This maneuver is often used to assess the condition of the heart, and may be performed as a treatment for cardiac arrhythmia or chest pain. The Valsalva maneuver works by increasing blood pressure, causing the heart to slow down temporarily. It should not be used with patients who suffer from severe coronary artery disease, or who have experienced a heart attack. Individuals often feel dizzy immediately after performing the Valsalva maneuver.

STATIC AND DYNAMIC STRETCHES

Muscle stretches can be described as either static or dynamic. A static stretch involves holding the muscle in an extended position for 30 seconds to a minute. In a static stretch, the muscle is eased into the stretched position. In a dynamic stretch, on the other hand, the muscle is brought into its stretched position through a series of short, violent motions. Dynamic stretches are also commonly referred to as ballistic stretches. The violent motions associated with dynamic stretching increase the risk of injury. At this time, few fitness experts recommend any form of dynamic or ballistic stretching.

FLEXIBILITY EXERCISES

Stretching exercises are a crucial part of every exercise program, and should be included in both the warm up and cool down sections. Flexibility exercises performed at the beginning of the workout, increase blood flow particularly to the ligaments and tendons that will be used more vigorously later in the workout. It is important to keep the stretches at the beginning of the workout gentle as unused tendons are more likely to be torn before the blood flow has been increased. Stretches should be performed with a smooth even motion without jerking. Although stretching may be accompanied by some discomfort whenever a sharp pain exists the stretch should be stopped immediately. Stretching is often based on individual ability so individuals should be encouraged only to stretch within their comfortable range of motion.

CARDIAC OUTPUT AND CONSUMPTION

The total volume of blood pumped from the heart is known as the cardiac output. Cardiac output can be calculated by multiplying stroke volume and heart rate in beats per minute. Stroke volume is simply the amount of blood that is pumped by an individual contraction of the heart. Oxygen consumption, meanwhile, is the measure of the amount of oxygen used by the body's cells. During exercise, the cells will be engaged in the production of ATP, necessitating greater levels of oxygen.

RESPIRATION AND AEROBIC CAPACITY

In exercise physiology, respiration is defined as the exchange of oxygen for carbon dioxide within the cells of the body. The oxygen that is inhaled is transferred by the blood to the outlying cells of the body, which then sends carbon dioxide back to the lungs to be expelled. The rate at which the lungs breathe in and out is known as ventilation. During exercise, the lungs expand and work more rapidly in order to increase ventilation. The ability of the blood to carry oxygen throughout the body is known as the aerobic capacity. Some individuals who suffer from respiratory disorders like asthma may have poor aerobic capacity even when breathing quickly and deeply.

BLOOD PRESSURE

Blood pressure is the measure of the force with which blood is circulated throughout the body. In order for the body to be efficient during exercise, there needs to be sufficient blood pressure to distribute oxygen rich blood to the muscle cells. Blood pressure is assessed with two measures: systolic blood pressure and diastolic blood pressure. The systolic blood pressure is the amount of force produced when the heart is contracted, and the expelled blood presses against the inside of the blood vessels. Diastolic blood pressure is the pressure of the blood in the arteries when the heart is not contracting. Although systolic blood pressure typically goes up during exercise, diastolic blood pressure remains fairly constant.

STEADY STATE

When the body is continuously meeting all of its oxygen needs during exercise, it is said to be in a steady state. It usually takes the body a few minutes to reach the steady state. When exercise is first initiated, the body takes a few minutes to adjust to the greater demands for oxygen. During this period, the anaerobic system helps to make up the oxygen deficit. When the intensity of the exercise is decreased, the body will be producing more oxygen than it needs. This extra energy production is used to expel lactic acid from the muscles.

CARDIORESPIRATORY TRAINING BENEFITS

Prolonged cardiorespiratory training will have many positive consequences. Most generally, people who adhere to an exercise program report lower levels of stress, anxiety, and depression. Regular exercise has also been shown to increase oxygen consumption, lower blood pressure, and increased resting metabolic rate. Regular cardiorespiratory training keeps the weight down, and leads to better self-image. Furthermore, individuals suffering from specific medical conditions like coronary artery disease, type 2 diabetes, or asthma report that regular exercise improves their symptoms.

HEART DISEASE

Coronary heart disease is a gradual diminishment of the blood to the heart, caused by the narrowing or blocking of the coronary artery. Severe coronary heart disease may result in myocardial infarction. When there is limited blood flow to the heart, the muscle cells will not receive enough oxygen. In other words, the lungs will be unable to distribute oxygen through the blood. Individuals are considered to be at special risk of coronary heart disease when they smoke, are obese, or suffer from high blood pressure. A lack of exercise, persistent anxiety, and a diet rich in saturated fats are all associated with the development of coronary heart disease.

HEART RATE, INTENSITY, AND OXYGEN

Exercise stimulates the heart rate to increase, delivering more oxygen to the cells so that aerobic glycolysis can be performed. The greater the intensity of the exercise, the greater the demand placed on the heart. The heart meets this demand by increasing both the stroke volume, and the amount of blood pumped by each heartbeat, and the number of beats per minute. Even after the intensity of the exercise climaxes and begins to diminish, the heart continues to deliver above-average levels of oxygen rich blood to the muscles. Aerobic glycolysis continues after high intensity exercise, preventing toxic materials from collecting in the muscles and causing cramps and fatigue.

ENVIRONMENTAL EFFECTS

It can be dangerous to exercise in either extreme heat or cold. When exercising in extreme heat, one must be sure to wear breathable clothing and consume large amounts of water. One should not wait until one is thirsty to drink. Individuals who will be exercising in direct sunlight should avoid wearing dark colors. When exercising in extremely cold weather, on the other hand, one should wear several light layers that can be taken off or put back on as necessary. In cold weather, blood tends to concentrate in the trunk of the body more than usual, so it is appropriate to extend the warm-up time. Also, even though one does not tend to get as thirsty in cold temperatures, it is important to drink fluids regularly.

At high altitudes, there is a lower concentration of oxygen in the atmosphere. This means that the lungs will have to work much harder in order to deliver oxygen to muscle cells. For this reason, one should always use caution when exercising at a high altitude. Individuals who have only recently entered this altitude should take one or two days to acclimate themselves. When exercising for the first time at a high altitude, one should exercise at a lower intensity than usual. If dizziness, nausea, or shortness of breath develops, one should immediately stop exercising. After a few days of low intensity exercise, most individuals will be fully acclimated.

NUTRIENT RECOMMENDATIONS

The United States government has issued a recommended daily allowance for the six categories of nutrients. The largest constituent of the human diet should be bread, cereal, rice, and pasta. It is recommended that individuals consume between six and 11 servings of these foods every day. The second-largest component of a healthy diet is the vegetable group, from which one should take three to five servings every day. One should consume two to four servings of fruits every day. One should consume two or three servings of meat, poultry, fish, dry beans, eggs, and nuts. Finally, one should consume less than one serving of fats, oils, and sweets a day.

Human beings get most of the vitamins that they need from the foods that they eat. Often times, however, people tried to increase their intake of a certain vitamin by consuming it in an isolated form. Indeed, increasing numbers of people are attempting to perfect their diet through the use of vitamins and nutritional supplements. In general, these substances are a helpful addition to the diet. However, it is possible to consume too many. The levels of vitamins and minerals are in a fine balance within the body; an overabundance of one vitamin or mineral may directly cause a deficiency in another. These days, most nutritionists recommend that individuals get the necessary vitamins and minerals from a healthy diet, rather than relying on pill vitamins and nutritional supplements.

CARDIORESPIRATORY SYSTEM

The efficiency with which blood and oxygen can be circulated throughout the body is the primary determinant for the individual's level of fitness. The heart is responsible for pumping oxygen rich blood throughout the body. Blood leaves the heart and travels to the peripheral areas of the body through the arteries; blood returns to the heart from these outlying areas through the veins. The veins bring blood into the right atrium of the heart, from which it flows into the right ventricle when the heart is relaxed. It then flows into the lungs where it is infused with oxygen and then sent back into the left atrium of the heart. The blood then flows into the left ventricle and out to the peripheral areas of the body.

EATING DISORDERS

Over the past decade, eating disorders have received an increased amount of scrutiny from the media and from health professionals. Specifically, attention is focused on the bulimia nervosa, anorexia nervosa, and binge eating. Bulimic individuals tend to eat a great deal of food and then purge by inducing themselves to vomit or by taking a laxative. Similarly, a binge eater consumes an abnormally large amount of food. Binge eaters, however, do not purge afterwards. Anorexic individuals, on the other hand, hardly eat at all. Fitness instructors should be especially aware of the signs of anorexia, because many anorexics will compulsively exercise in an effort to drive their weight even farther down. All of these eating disorders are typically the result of an erroneously negative body image.

SPECIAL DIETARY NEEDS

It is increasingly common for individuals with specific medical conditions to have special dietary needs. Any individual who is participating in an exercise program should be sure to regulate his or her levels of iron, sugar, fat, and vitamin D. Any diabetics in the fitness class should be well trained in checking their own blood sugar level. Anemics, on the other hand, should be sure that their iron levels are high enough to permit them to participate in the exercise program. In any situation where a fitness instructor feels that a participant's diet is affecting his or her performance in class, the instructor should refer that participant to a certified nutritionist.

CHOLESTEROL, LIPOPROTEINS AND TRIGLYCERIDES

Cholesterol, lipoproteins, and triglycerides are all kinds of fat stored in the body. Triglycerides are fats that reside in the blood. If the level of triglycerides in the blood becomes too high, it is possible for the arteries to become blocked. This can result in a heart attack or in coronary artery disease. Furthermore, blockages in the arteries can make vigorous exercise dangerous. Cholesterol is the blanket name given to two different kinds of lipoproteins. High-density lipoproteins are important for the body's function, in so far as they speed nutrients from one location in the body to another. Low-density lipoproteins, on the other hand, have the potential to block arteries and inhibit blood flow.

PRINCIPLES OF MOVEMENT

Biomechanics is the science of the anatomical principles of movement. The basic principles of this field are the three laws of motion identified by Sir Isaac Newton. The law of inertia states that body is at rest or in motion will tend to stay at rest or in motion unless acted upon by some other force. The law of acceleration states that the force acting on the body is equal to the mass of the body multiplied by its acceleration. The law of action and reaction declares that when two bodies come into contact with one another their impact on one another is equal in magnitude and opposite in direction.

PAR-Q

For most healthy individuals, there is little to no risk of an adverse effect occurring when engaging in physical activity. The PAR-Q is a screening tool designed to identify the relatively small percentage of adults for whom physical activity might pose a health risk or those who should seek medical clearance from a physician prior to engaging in activity to help mitigate such risk.

Physical Activity Readiness Questionnaire (PAR-Q)	
Has your doctor ever said you have heart trouble?	Yes/No
Do you frequently have pains in your heart and chest?	Yes/No
Do you often feel faint or have spells of severe dizziness?	Yes/No
Has a doctor ever said your blood pressure was too high?	Yes/No
Has your doctor ever told you that you have a bone or joint problem such as arthritis that has been aggravated by exercise, or might be made worse with exercise?	Yes/No
Is there a good physical reason not mentioned here why you should not follow an activity program even if you wanted to?	Yes/No
Are you over age 65 and not accustomed to vigorous exercise?	Yes/No
If you answered YES to one or more questions:	Yes/No
If you have not recently done so, consult with your personal physician by telephone or in person before increasing your physical activity and/or taking a fitness test.	
If you answered NO to all questions, you have reasonable assurance that graduated mild to moderate exercise is safe to perform.	
If you answered PAR-Q accurately, you have reasonable assurance of your present suitability for exercise.	

BORG RATING SCALE

The Borg Scale is used to assess an individuals's rating of his or her perceived exertion during physical activity. The participant selects a number from 6 to 20 that best describes his or her level of perceived exertion. On the Borg Scale, a value of 6 indicates absolutely no physical exertion, 9 corresponds to "very light" exercise such as slow and comfortable walking, 11 is light, 13 corresponds to "somewhat hard" exercise that still feels fine to continue, 15 is hard or heavy work, 17 is very strenuous, and 20 denotes maximal exertion.

THE KARVONEN FORMULA

Maximal heart rate (MHR) is first estimated using the fomula 220-age. Resting heart rate (RHR) is subtracted from the calculated MHR to find heart rate reserve (HRR). HRR is multiplied by .50 and .85 to get the minimum and maximum of THRR intensity, respectively. RHR is added back in the fomula.

Recommendations:

Beginners or indivduals with low fitness levels: 50% - 60% HRR

Individuals of average fitness level: 60% - 70% HRR

Highly fit: 75% - 85% HRR

MEASURING BODY FAT
BODY FAT IS USUALLY TESTED IN 4 DIFFERENT WAYS.

- Hydrostatic weighing (Immersion): This test is considered the "gold standard" for body fat assessment. The individual is weighed on land and then submerged under water in a tank where weight is again measured. After correcting for water density, the loss of weight as appreciated underwater is used to assess water displacement and percent body fat.
  - Pros: When done correctly, provides the most accurate measurement.
  - Cons: Although this procedure is sometimes available at large universities, it requires a lot of equipment. It is also time-consuming, uncomfortable, quite involved, and is affected by the individual's consumption before the test and ability to expel air from his or her lungs.
- Impedance: Body fat percentage is calculated using a device that measures the electrical impedance between certain areas of the body, usually the fingers and toes.
- Pinch test: Calipers are used to measure the thickness of the tissue pinched from the body area.
  - Pros: Fairly reliable, especially when many sites are measured. Most gyms have a caliper available.
  - Cons: Individuals may feel embarrassed or self-conscious when baring skin and having fat pinched. Results may be quite inaccurate with an inexperienced evaluator.
  - Cons: May be embarrassing to have someone pinch your fat. If the person is inexperienced the results may be very inaccurate.

PNF Stretches

Hold-relax	This stretching technique starts with a passive pre-stretch held for 10 seconds at the point that a tight sensation is felt. After the 10 seconds has elapsed, the patient is told to a try to extend the hip while the therapist provides resistance. This causes an isometric muscle contraction, which is held for 6 seconds. Next, the patient is instructed to relax and perform a passive stretch held comfortably for 30 seconds. This final passive stretch should experience a greater range of motion because of autogenic inhibition.
Hold-relax stretch with agonist contraction	This technique is identical to that of "hold-relax" during its first two phases. However, if differs by instructing the patient to perform a concentric contraction of the agonist and in the final 30-second passive stretch phase. The final stretch should achieve a greater range of motion because of both autogenic and reciprocal inhibition of the muscles.
Contract-relax	This stretching technique also starts with a passive pre-stretch held for 10 seconds at the point when a tight sensation is felt. Then, the patient is instructed to extend the hip against therapist-applied manual resistance, allowing a concentric muscle contraction through the joint's full range of motion, instead of than maintaining an isometric contraction of the hamstring muscle. Next, the patient relaxes and the therapist applies a passive hip flexion stretch force for 30 seconds. The range of motion achieved should be greater because of autogenic inhibition.

WEIGHT LOSS APPROACHES

It is appropriate for overweight or obese individuals to work towards weight loss. However, there are different ways of achieving this change. An immediate, severe restriction of food consumption, otherwise known as a crash diet, is an extremely unhealthy way to achieve weight loss. Furthermore, sudden weight loss typically comes from a decrease in muscle mass, which has the effect of decreasing the metabolism and making it difficult to lose weight subsequently. Losing weight through excessive exercising is also unhealthy. Fitness instructors should always promote weight loss through a combination of healthy diet and regular exercise. Fitness instructor should constantly remind participants that sustained weight loss is a long-term proposition.

ANATOMICAL POSITION

The anatomy of the human body can be divided into three different planes: the sagittal, transverse, and frontal planes. The sagittal plane divides the body into right and left sections. The transverse plane divides the body into upper and lower sections. The frontal plane divides the body into front and back sections. Any movement in the sagittal plane that decreases the angle between the anterior surfaces of the moving bones is called flexion, while any movement that increases this angle is called extension. The word rotation is used to describe movements that occur in the transverse plane. Such rotations can be either internal or external, depending on their direction. Any movement in the frontal plane that is away from the midline is called abduction, while movement towards the midline is known as adduction.

RANGE OF CURVATURES

A properly curved spine will have two minor anterior curves in the lower back and neck. There will also be a small posterior curve in the thoracic area. There are a few common deviant curvatures, however. Individuals suffering from kyphosis will have an exaggerated posterior curve in the spine. Individuals with scoliosis will have an exaggerated lateral curvature of the spine. Individuals with lordosis will have an exaggerated anterior curvature of the spine. Lordosis typically occurs in the neck or in the lower back. A fitness instructor should be vigilant for the signs of deviant curvature in the spine, and should refer individuals suffering from these abnormalities to a medical specialist.

KINDS OF MUSCLES

There are three basic kinds of muscles: agonists, antagonists, and synergists. An agonist is a muscle that initiates movement. When an agonist contracts, it allows the joint to pass through its normal range of motion. An antagonist muscle, on the other hand, acts in opposition to the agonist. The antagonist muscle restores the joint to its normal arrangement. Agonists and antagonists are usually found in pairs. A synergist muscle, finally, is a muscle which either performs or assists in performing the motion performed by an agonist. Occasionally agonist muscles are too strong for their own good; in these cases, the synergist muscle restrains the agonist.

ACTIONS OF MAJOR MUSCLES

The gluteus maximus muscle is responsible for extending and rotating the hip. The hamstrings, located on the posterior thigh, also help to extend the hip joint. The abdominal muscles, both internal and external, allow the spine to move laterally. The rectus abdominal muscle allows the trunk to bend forward and backward. The movements of the arms and shoulders are controlled by the deltoids, triceps, biceps, and trapezius muscles. The movements of the legs and feet are mainly controlled by the posterior tibialis, soleus, and gastrocnemius muscles. Finally, the rotation of the shoulders and back is controlled by the latissimus dorsi muscles.

Group Instructional Methods

CLASS OBJECTIVES

It is helpful if the fitness instructor sets objectives both for each individual and for the class as a whole. Furthermore, the instructor should set goals for each lesson as well as goals for the fitness program as a whole. These goals should be challenging but realistic. It is best to develop the fitness goals at the beginning of an exercise program in consultation with the class as a whole and with each participant in the class individually. Then, as the class moves forward, the instructor will be able to select exercise activities tailored to the individual and collective goals of the class.

CHOOSING CLASS EXERCISES

The exercise activities selected for class should always be chosen with the fitness objectives in mind. A fitness instructor wants to include all the activities that promote the fitness objectives, without selecting moves that are too intense or redundant. For instance, it is not necessary to perform three or four different stretches for the same muscle or group of muscles. Also, some complex aerobic routines may be too advanced for beginning participants. A fitness instructor should select the activities that will challenge the participants in the class, without discouraging them from future participation.

SLOW-TO-FAST STRATEGY

One of the strategies used by fitness instructors for teaching complicated exercise routines is known as the slow-to-fast strategy. Instructors who use this strategy start a new routine very slowly, and gradually increase speed as the participants in the class move from cognitive understanding, to associative understanding, and finally to autonomous understanding. Common sense suggests that individuals will be better able to make self-corrections when they learn a new maneuver slowly. One consideration to take into account when using the slow-to-fast strategy is that it will immediately decrease the intensity of the exercise, and so is probably inappropriate for the peak times in the exercise class. For this reason, many instructors use the slow-to-fast strategy to teach new maneuvers at the beginning of each class.

PERSONAL FACTORS

Some personality characteristics make it less likely that an individual will adhere to an exercise program over a long period of time. Smokers, obese individuals, and individuals of a low socioeconomic class are unlikely to adhere to an exercise program for several months. However, individuals who have participated in exercise programs before, non-smokers, and individuals with a high level of self-confidence are likely to stick with an exercise program over the long haul. A fitness instructor needs to be cognizant of which individuals are at risk of dropping out of an exercise program. These individuals may require extra encouragement.

CUES

Fitness instructors use verbal and visual cues to instruct the class. For instance, instructors will use verbal cues to alert the participants to a change in the exercise activity. Physical cues are often used to provide specific instruction for performing complicated activities. Although pointing at participants may be effective for getting their attention, the instructor should be sure not to bring undue attention to members of the class who may feel insecure about their performance. If the instructor is going to be using idiosyncratic verbal cues, he or she should explain them before the beginning of the class. An example of this sort of verbal cue is when an instructor has a catchphrase that he or she uses to get the class's attention quickly or to denote a change in activity.

Because so much of fitness instruction is teaching complex patterns of movement, it makes sense that visual cues will often be the preferred method of instruction. The most common kind of visual cue that will be used in the fitness class will be a demonstration of the activity of the classes to perform. Such a demonstration should always begin slowly, so that participants can totally study the activity. A physical demonstration of a complex exercise activity should be accompanied by verbal cues describing the technique. Some of the other common visual cues used by physical fitness instructors are pointing and waving. A fitness instructor may use these cues to point out specific errors in technique, or simply to get the attention of the class.

Although verbal cues should be used throughout the exercise class, a fitness instructor should try to keep them as short and efficient as possible. For one thing, it is not easy to talk a great deal while exercising at a moderate intensity. An instructor will quickly learn to drink plenty of water during each exercise class, and to deliver verbal cues from positions that do not constrict the lungs or abdomen. In general, the instructor wants to maintain a normal tone of voice that is upbeat and encouraging.

PRACTICE STYLE

One of the common styles of instruction used by fitness teachers is known as the practice style. Instructors who use the practice style give their participants a great deal of freedom to make adjustments during the exercise class. The instructor will circulate throughout the room providing personalized feedback to the participants, and the participants will be allowed to adjust the intensity and quantity of their exercise. This technique is good when all the participants in the class have moderate experience in the fitness training, and are capable of judging their own performance. The practice style of instruction is not appropriate for beginning classes.

RECIPROCAL STYLE

One of the common styles of instruction used by fitness teachers is the reciprocal style. The style of instruction is useful when the participants in the fitness class are too numerous to be given personalized feedback. In the reciprocal style of instruction, the participants in the class are divided into pairs, and instructed to monitor and provide feedback to one another. A fitness instructor should take care not to place inexperienced members of the class in partnerships with one another. Also, the fitness instructor should provide specific instruction to the participants as to what they should be looking for in their partner's performance.

SELF-CHECK STYLE

One of the common styles of instruction used by fitness teachers is the self-check style. In this style of teaching, the instructor has all the participants in the class monitor their own progress. This may involve checking heart rate, recording measurements, or filling out some brief documentation. This kind of instruction is especially effective during exercises that can be easily measured, as for instance muscular strength and endurance training exercises, and cardiorespiratory exercises. The self-check style of instruction should only be used when all the participants in the class are experienced.

INCLUSION STYLE

When the participants in an exercise class represent a wide range of fitness levels, the instructor may want to incorporate the inclusion style of instruction. The instructor who uses the inclusion style demonstrates an array of different techniques and activities that can be performed by individuals at different fitness levels. One example of this kind of instruction is the presentation of alternative stretches for those individuals who cannot perform the basic stretches that have been taught. The inclusion style of instruction is necessary when the class has a particularly broad range of fitness levels. It is time consuming however, and so should not be used unless it is absolutely necessary.

REPETITION REDUCTION STRATEGY

One of the common instruction strategies used in exercise classes is known as the repetition reduction strategy. To use this strategy, the instructor simply increases the number of repetitions by two or three times. For instance, an aerobics instructor who is trying to teach a pattern of two steps forward and one kick left might first teach a pattern of four steps forward and two kicks last. This teaching strategy helps the participants in the class to achieve a quick cognitive understanding of the move. The repetition reduction strategy is most effective when it is set to music.

SPATIAL STRATEGY

One of the common instruction strategies used in exercise classes is known as the spatial strategy. A teacher using this strategy will explain the proper technique for a maneuver one body part at a time. In other words, when describing an elaborate dance sequence a teacher would begin by describing the movement of the right foot and leg, then the left foot and leg, and then the left and right arms, respectively. A teacher using the spatial strategy may have the participants in the class practice the movements of one part of the body in isolation before moving on to other parts. Many teachers of complex exercise routines find that the spatial strategy helps students to gradually assimilate a complicated maneuver. Instructors may either work from the bottom of the body up or from the top down.

PART-TO-WHOLE STRATEGY

One of the common teaching strategies employed by fitness instructors for teaching complex movements is called the part-to-whole strategy. A teacher using the part part-to-whole strategy will break a complicated move down into simple parts which can be taught independently. After the first part of the move has been mastered, the class can move on to the second part, and so on. By building knowledge incrementally, the teacher maintains the confidence of the class and ensures that each component of the complex maneuver is performed correctly. This strategy for instruction is especially effective with beginning level classes.

SIMPLE-TO-COMPLEX STRATEGY

One of the common instructional strategies used by fitness instructors when teaching complex movements is known as the simple to complex teaching strategy. This strategy is simply consists of beginning with the simplest parts of a complex maneuver, and gradually increasing the complexity. For example, an instructor teaching dance moves that require elaborate gestures with both arms might begin by instructing the participants in the movements of only one arm. After the participants have mastered the movements of the right arm, say, they can begin to learn the movements for the left arm.

EXERCISE CLASS FORMAT

The basic exercise class has six parts. Before the class begins, the instructor should become familiar with the level of fitness of all the participants, and the participants should become familiar with the class environment. During the warm-up, the body temperature of the participants should be gradually raised so that the heart and lungs can be accustomed to an increased workload. Once all the participants have warmed up, the class can begin cardiorespiratory work. After approximately 30 minutes of cardiorespiratory work, the class can begin muscular strength and endurance exercises. When these are complete, the class can work on flexibility as part of the cool down sections of the exercise class. This last section allows the blood flow to restore normal levels.

DOMAINS OF LEARNING

Basic educational psychology suggests that there are three domains of learning: the motor, affective, and cognitive modes. Motor learning is the kind of learning most often associated with fitness programs. Learning a new exercise routine is an example of motor learning. Affective learning is learning that has to do with the emotions. A successful fitness instructor will need to manage the emotions of the participants in his or her class to derive the best possible benefit to them. Finally, cognitive learning is the kind of intellectual information acquiring that most people associate with academic learning. Fitness instructors should supplement their motor and affective approaches by telling the participants in an exercise class, the intellectual reasons for each activity as well as the benefits and consequences of persistent exercise.

The job of a fitness instructor is to guide the participants in an exercise class from the cognitive stage of learning motor skills through the autonomous stage of learning skills. Participants are likely to become frustrated during the cognitive stage of learning, because remembering all the steps of a complex skill requires a great deal of effort. The fitness instructor should pay special attention to maintaining the morale of the class during the difficult cognitive stage of learning. Extremely complicated physical maneuvers should be broken down into small components which are learned individually. As the participants in the class are practicing the steps of the maneuver, the fitness instructor should give specific guidance and positive constructive feedback.

MUSICAL TERMS

In order to effectively incorporate music into the fitness program a fitness instructor needs to know a few basic pieces of musical terminology. The beat of the music, otherwise known as the rhythm, is simply the regular pulsation, usually indicated by the drums. An accented beat is known as a downbeat, while an unaccented beat is known as an upbeat. One complete cycle of down beats and upbeats is called a measure. The number of beats in each measure is the meter of the music. The first beat of the group is called the "pickup". The number of beats per minute is also known as the tempo of the music.

SELECTING CHOREOGRAPHY

When developing the choreography for an exercise class, a fitness instructor should keep in mind the fitness level and coordination of the participants. Many dance motions require flexibility and muscular strength that may be beyond the capability of some students. Also, some violent dance motions may put undue strain on the joints of the body. Stretches that are performed as part of the class choreography should be smooth and even, with no bouncing. Finally, a fitness instructor wants to ensure that the choreography for the exercise class uses muscle groups on both sides of the body.

The methods of choreography employed by fitness instructors can be described as either freestyle or structured. Freestyle choreography is improvised during the course of a class. Instructors who are very familiar with their students, and have a great deal of experience themselves, may be quite successful using freestyle choreography. Structured choreography, on the other hand, is planned before the beginning of the class. Fitness instructors who are just beginning their careers, or are unfamiliar with the fitness levels of the class, should probably make a structured choreography plan before the beginning of each class. Many teachers find that the best system is to create a structured choreography plan, and then deviate from it when necessary.

EXERCISE ADHERENCE FACTORS

There are a number of aspects of an exercise program that can affect adherence by the participants. Some individuals will be less likely to attend a fitness class that occurs at a certain time of day, for instance after lunch or early in the morning. Some participants will not be able to regularly attend classes that last longer than an hour. Also, some participants will be unlikely to attend a class if they feel that they are either too fit or not fit enough. In order to encourage adherence to the exercise plan, a fitness instructor should be familiar with the personal needs and fitness requirements of all the individuals in the class.

There are a number of environmental factors that may affect the appearance of the participants in an exercise class to the fitness plan. An exercise room that is clean and bright will encourage participants to return. If the room is too cold or is otherwise uncomfortable, however, participants will be less likely to come back. Perhaps the most important aspect of the fitness environment, though, is the rapport between the fitness instructor and the participants. Instructors who are supportive and positive with their students tend to have higher levels of adherence. Instructors should always be professional and punctual to their classes, so as to encourage similar virtues in the students.

MOTIVATION

Motivation is characterized by the following three aspects:

- Qualities and activities that concern human behavior
- The stimulus or cause directing behavior toward a specific goal
- The manner and method in which this behavior is maintained

MOTIVATION PROCESSES:

- Intrinsic Reward: an intangible reward, such as praise and improved self-esteem.
- Extrinsic Reward: a tangible reward, such as a trophy or favorite treat.
- Punishment: the act of delivering an aversive consequence in response to a poor or undesirable behavior, as a way to deter or decrease the likelihood of repeating the behavior.
- Extinction: ignoring or avoiding reinforcing the specific behavior.
- Positive Reinforcement: the aim of positive reinforcement is to optimize the likelihood that a desired behavior will occur in the future. This is achieved by providing a positive or attractive stimulus (a "reward" of sorts) after successful completion of the operant response (the desired behavior).

Unfortunately, many individuals will be unable to stick with an exercise program over a long period of time. In order to minimize the number of dropouts, a fitness instructor needs to know how to maintain high motivation in the class participants. One sure way to discourage the participants in the class is by setting unrealistic expectations. The goals for the class should be challenging but realistic. At all times, the instructor should be reminding the participants of the positive benefits of exercise, especially those that are not visible to the naked eye. Although it is inevitable that some of the fitness work will be strenuous and difficult, as much as possible, the instructor should endeavor to make classes fun.

One of the most effective ways to maintain motivation in the participants in an exercise class is by setting challenging and realistic goals. These goals should be created by the fitness instructor in consultation with each participant. Individuals may have short and long term goals regarding muscular strength, endurance, flexibility, and weight loss. The fitness goals should always be written down and reviewed regularly. Some of the short-term goals that many participants in an exercise class have are to be able to achieve a complicated dance sequence, to endure high-intensity cardiorespiratory exercise for a longer period of time, or to demonstrate increased flexibility.

One of the most important things a fitness instructor can do is to provide positive feedback and reinforcement to all the participants in the class. Studies indicate that students consistently perform better when they are given continual encouragement. It is important, however, that the praise given by the instructor be specific. To this end, the instructor should maintain detailed records of performance. This way, the instructor will be able to point out specific areas in which each participant has improved. It is common for participants to become discouraged and forget how much progress they have made during the course of an exercise program. The job of the instructor is to remind each participant of long-term goals and progress.

A fitness instructor should never discourage participants by making the exercise class too difficult, boring, or complicated. Instead, the instructor should maintain a positive environment atmosphere in the class. To make sure that the class environment is acceptable for all the participants in the class, the instructor should regularly confer with the participants on possible music and variations in the exercise program. Students will be more enthusiastic about an exercise class in which they feel they have an influence. The instructor should regularly ask for feedback from the participants, for instance on which areas of the class are considered to be successful and which are less effective. Finally, the instructor should endeavor to maintain a positive attitude as much as possible.

Although the fitness instructor should seek to minimize discomfort for participants during an exercise class, it is to be expected that there will be some degree of discomfort during strenuous exercise. A fitness instructor needs to be able to distinguish between normal levels of pain and pain that may indicate injury. A fitness instructor should take seriously any complaints of pain made by the participants. However, a fitness instructor should make sure that that all participants can distinguish between signs of serious health problems and the normal results of vigorous exercise. Any participants who complain of chest pain, dizziness, or lightheadedness should immediately decrease intensity.

Many fitness instructors find that they can increase adherence to an exercise program by using cues and reminders. An example of such a reminder might be a regular newsletter detailing the activities of the class, or a flyer posted at the exercise facility. A fitness instructor might make copies of the music used during the fitness class, so that participants can remind themselves of the fitness environment while at home or at work.

One way, too, that many fitness instructors encourage adherence to fitness programs is by encouraging social supports among participants. A fitness instructor can then encourage each participant to call those participants that he or she knows to make sure that they will be attending class. The participants in the class can also get together to discuss their fitness goals and the state of the class in general. Many beginning participants would benefit by having an experienced mentor within the class. This mentor would be responsible for making sure the new participant attends all the classes and keeps efficient documentation of progress. In order to encourage the social supports, the fitness instructor they suggest that participants invite their friends and family to join the exercise class.

One of the most important things a fitness instructor can do is encourage camaraderie among the participants. If the participants in the fitness class make strong social contacts with one another, they will be more likely to adhere to the fitness program. A good way to initiate this process is to have the members of the class introduce themselves to one another at the beginning of the fitness program. During the warm-up and cool down portions of the class, the instructor may encourage the students to talk amongst themselves. The instructor should not allow any members of the class to diminish morale by complaining or criticizing other participants.

Physical fitness instructors should always take care to emphasize the positive aspects of the participants' performance. Many individuals will begin in an exercise class with trepidation and self-doubt. It is the job of a fitness instructor to allay these concerns, and demonstrably show to all the participants that progress can be made if honest effort is given. It is inevitable that some aspects of the fitness program will be less enjoyable than others; a fitness instructor should take care to emphasize the positive consequences of seemingly difficult work. The fitness instructor should take care to remind the participants of the long-term fitness goals, so as to ensure that participants maintain the high level of effort.

Over the course of a long fitness program, it is inevitable that there will be some interruptions. In order to minimize the damage done by these interruptions, the fitness instructor should take care to warn participants. For instance, if a fitness instructor is aware that he or she will have to miss one or more classes, then he or she should introduce the substitute instructor to the class at the earliest convenience. If the instructor knows that he or she will have to be absent for a long period of time, it is especially important to cultivate self-monitoring skills and the participants. Also, it is important for the instructor to notify participants of any significant changes in the structure or contents of the exercise class. In the event the class must be canceled for some unforeseen reason, it is a good idea for participants to have a basic routine that they can perform individually.

In order for the participants in an exercise class to reach their fitness goals, they need to maintain a healthy lifestyle outside of the class environment. A well-trained fitness instructor will be informed on the issues of nutrition and weight control, and will be able to provide specific guidelines to the participants in the class. It may be helpful for the instructor to provide lists of appropriate foods for the participants in the class, as well as to provide forms on which participants can document their food and drink consumption. The achievement of long-term goals in the fitness class should be based not only on physical performance within the class environment, but on adherence to nutritional requirements outside of class.

Many of the participants in an exercise class will begin with a self-conscious and insecure mindset. It is important for the fitness instructor to not let this attitude deteriorate into defeatism. Temporary setbacks in the fitness class should not be allowed to degenerate into long term problems. In order to minimize defeatism in the fitness class, the instructor should always accentuate the positive aspects of performance. Even those participants who are struggling the most with the requirements of the exercise class should be given regular positive feedback.

BODY IMAGE

The self-consciousness that many participants in an exercise class will feel is the result of their negative body image. Women, in particular, are subject to bad self-image as a result of the ideals put forth by the media. Unfortunately, many women believe that they must be shaped like supermodels in order to be attractive. A fitness instructor must take care to foster a positive self-image in all the participants in an exercise class. Whenever a participant in the class expresses negative feelings about his or her body, a fitness instructor should be sure to contradict these harmful statements.

Many beginning fitness students will come to class with an unrealistically negative body image. The job of a fitness instructor is to encourage students to view themselves charitably. Participants in an exercise class should also be aware that making great changes in physical appearance takes time, and cannot be accomplished through brief, high intensity work. If the instructor feels that an individual is exercising too hard or too often, the instructor should speak to that individual privately about the dangers of excessive exercise.

ANKLE AND/OR HAND WEIGHTS

Many common aerobic routines will become more intense with the addition of ankle and hand weights. These waves increase the resistance and require more strength and endurance from the muscles. Ankle and hand weights should not exceed 3 pounds, to avoid placing undue weight on the joints. Also, participants who are inexperienced with hand weights should take care to monitor their heart rate while wearing them. Ankle and hand weights are primarily designed to promote muscular endurance and cardiorespiratory strength, and not to actually build muscle strength.

USING CUES

When leading a class through a muscular strength and endurance program, a fitness instructor should pay special attention to those aspects of technique that can affect the success of the exercise. Specifically, the instructor should be sensitive to errors of technique that can result in injury. For instance, there are many upper body exercises that are performed while standing. In these exercises, students should stand with their knees slightly bent. Also, there are very few standing exercises in which the spine is bent. When lifting objects from the ground, the majority of the work should be done with the knees rather than the back. Muscular strength and endurance exercises should always be performed slowly and through the entire range of motion.

A fitness instructor uses verbal posture cues to ensure that participants maintain proper form during each component of an exercise class. If students do not maintain proper posture, they put themselves at risk of injury. The most common posture during an exercise class is standing. The correct standing posture is with the shoulders positioned directly above the hips, which are directly above the knees. The feet should be shoulder-width apart, and the chest should be extended out, giving a gentle convex curve to the lower back. When sitting, participants should try to avoid slumping their shoulders, and should strive to keep the back straight.

Alignment cues are verbal or visual instructions given to the participants in an exercise class regarding their posture or position during certain exercises. Alignment cues are especially important during those exercises which, if performed incorrectly, can result in injury. Although the fitness instructor should take care to respect the personal boundaries of all the participants, he or she may need to put his or her hands on the participants in order to effectively demonstrate proper positioning. A fitness instructor should always be aware that some students may not be physically capable of attaining the proper positioning for an exercise. These participants should simply not participate in this segment of the exercise class.

FEEDBACK

An effective fit instructor will provide constant feedback to all the participants in the class. Participants should receive feedback whether they are performing well or performing poorly. As much as possible, feedback should be specific and impersonal. Feedback is most helpful when it specifically pertains to the exercise that is being performed. Fitness instructors should be especially sure to provide positive feedback to beginning students. Continuous feedback, both positive and negative, helps the participants in an exercise class monitor their own performance and become conscious of progress.

Throughout an exercise class, the instructor should use verbal cues to provide guidance to students. Verbal cues are most effective when the instructor is familiar with each participant's level of fitness. Also, the instructor needs to be able to clearly and concisely describe the technique for each of the exercises in the class. It is important for the instructor to build a good rapport with all of his or her students so that students will feel comfortable approaching instructor with questions.

Group Leadership and Class Management

SPECIAL POPULATIONS

A special population is a group of people that have either a common health problem or impairment or a particular characteristic that makes it necessary to alter the general rules of training in order to accommodate his or her needs.

The basic concepts that ACE teaches are meant to apply to adults who are generally healthy and can cope with the basic rigors of a workout regimen. Others do not fit into this general mold. Some special populations include:

- Young persons or those who have not finished growing physically
- The elderly or those older than age 65
- Those with osteoporosis or low bone density
- Pregnant women
- Overweight clients whose body mass index (BMI) exceeds the normal healthy range but does not exceed 30
- Obese clients whose BMI is 30 or more
- Diabetic clients
- Arthritic clients
- Persons with hypertension
- Those suffering from coronary heart disease (CHD)

Members of special populations have either a common health problem or impairment or particular characteristic that makes it necessary to alter the general rules of training in order to accommodate their needs.

For example, children or adolescents have not completed their growing cycles and, while often having superior cardiorespiratory capabilities, should be monitored in their strength-training routines.

Likewise, those with osteoporosis, a disease characterized by low bone density, need to engage in weight-bearing exercise in order to help increase their bone density, but it must be done in a manner that keeps physical limitations in mind in order to keep the client safe.

Pregnant women can also work out effectively, but a fitness instructor needs to be aware of several important physiological changes that take place during gestation. These include the fact that a pregnant woman has a much higher blood volume as well as a general loosening of the body's ligaments, both of which may affect her stability and ability to maintain certain positions.

YOUNG PEOPLE

Health and fitness professionals often work with younger clients in varying contexts. A member of this population can be anywhere between grade-school age (from 5 or 6 to 12), through adolescence (12 to 18), and up to young adulthood (approximately 21).

Younger clients are distinct from the average adult population and cannot be trained according to standard adult parameters. Many training guidelines for young people deal with physical-education–type training or youth sports. But currently, given that obesity is a much more widespread problem than in previous generations, the demand for regular training designed for young people has increased dramatically. Younger people need at least 20 minutes of activity that increases the heart rate at least three times each week, with an hour being ideal.

OXYGEN CONSUMPTION

A young person's oxygen consumption rate, or VO2, is very similar to an adult's, when height and weight are calibrated appropriately. This means that young people are generally just as capable, if not more capable, as an adult of performing cardiorespiratory training activities that require some level of endurance. Younger children (6 to 12) should be able to tolerate vigorous activity for 30 to 60 minutes up to every day of the week.

Increases in training volume should not go beyond 10 percent of the previous week's activity. For example, if a young person engages in 30 minutes of exercise three times per week, or 90 minutes total for the week, the following week should add only nine additional minutes, or three minutes per session, in order to safely progress.

SUBMAXIMAL OXYGEN

A young person's submaximal oxygen consumption exceeds that of the average adult for activities such as walking, jogging, and sprinting. This means that younger people have a higher risk for tiring and/or overheating in vigorous exercises.

Trainers should make sure that youth clients are well hydrated and do not overexert themselves with high-intensity exercise, particularly when the weather is hot and humid. Exercise that increases the heart rate can safely be enjoyed at least three times a week for at least 20 minutes. Anaerobic activity that goes beyond ten seconds at a stretch is not usually advisable.

GLYCOLIC ENZYME LEVELS

A young person has lower levels of glycolic enzymes than the average adult, which means that he or she would have a lower tolerance for very intense activities that are anaerobic in nature, lasting more than 10 seconds and up to 90 seconds.

A weight-training regimen should include the following:

A variety of between 8 and 10 different exercises is chosen. One or two sets of each exercise should be performed, consisting of 8 to 12 repetitions. Repetitions should not go beyond 20 when endurance is the goal and should not exceed about 6 when strength is the goal. When performing these exercises, the trainer should make sure that the client is using proper form and is completely controlling the movements so as not to put excessive strain on the joints.

RATE OF SWEATING

A young person has a lower ability to handle extremes in environment, and extra caution should be taken when exercising in hot and humid environments. Time should be allotted for both a warm-up and cool-down in order to give the young person's body enough time to adjust to environmental factors.

In order to increase tolerance, repetitions should be added to a workout routine first, and then additional weight is added later for each exercise in the routine.

Be sure the youth client is properly hydrated, and observe for visual cues of diminishing performance that might signal distress or overheating. Younger clients may not be as body aware or as able to communicate physical distress as adults.

WEIGHT TRAINING

While there is a common idea that weight training is not appropriate for youth clients, research has shown that it is not harmful and can have positive benefits. In fact, research has demonstrated that weight training actually has a lower risk of causing a serious injury than many of the different kinds of organized sports that young people participate in.

While there are some risks involved with resistance training, namely danger of pulls and tears, these can in large part be avoided with proper training and effective monitoring. It is also important to perform a movement assessment much like the one given to an adult client in order to determine a youth client's capabilities prior to beginning a systematic, progressive weight-training regimen.

MOVEMENT ASSESSMENT

A modified weight-training assessment can be performed for a youth client by having him or her perform 10 squats and 10 push-ups (these can be modified for a female client or lower-strength client). Be sure to gauge all the of the appropriate kinetic-chain checkpoints that are standard to all ACE fitness assessments. The results will help inform the trainer as to which exercises will be the best for the particular client and also which specific areas to monitor carefully during training sessions.

Weight training for youth clients can increase strength, bone density, and general coordination.

The health and fitness professional should take into account the fitness assessment of the youth client and other general background information when designing an appropriate resistance-training program. Taking a client from the stabilization level into the higher phases will depend on physical ability, the client's overall ability to handle the regimen, and, of course, the recommendation of his or her doctor.

Another important factor is that training for the youth client should be engaging and fun. In order to maintain motivation and interest and encourage a lifelong interest in fitness, keeping the routines fun is vitally important.

BASIC GUIDELINES

Youth clients should have a fun training experience with safe activities that are adequately supervised by an adult. Games, sports, walking, running, water sports, and even weight training are good types of exercise for youth clients. Training can be engaged in from three to five times per week for at least 20 minutes, with an hour being ideal. A movement assessment should observe kinetic-chain checkpoints while the youth client performs 10 push-ups and 10 squats. High-level training requires physical ability and enough maturity to understand and duplicate instructions safely.

SENIORS

Seniors are defined as those who are 65 years of age and older. Given that the population of seniors is growing exponentially now that the baby boomer generation is maturing, the need for training with health and fitness professionals who understand how to safely and effectively work with members of this population is great.

Keeping fit can dramatically impact the quality of life a senior will have in later years. Training can help improve bone density and maintain coordination and overall muscle tone. Many primary functions of the body decline with age, including:

- Elasticity of tissues
- Muscle mass
- Bone density
- Blood volume output
- Neuromuscular coordination
- Maximum heart rate

DISEASES OR CHRONIC CONDITIONS

Common chronic conditions associated with older age include lower bone density (osteoporosis), arthritis, overweight or obesity, and back problems. These problems can themselves be classified as special populations, and a health and fitness trainer should note specific problems a client may have and cross-reference these with guidelines for any other special population.

However, just because a senior has a different body condition than a younger adult does not mean there is a problem. An older adult may have a higher resting blood pressure measurement, but this may not indicate that something is wrong that must be compensated for significantly in training. As with all clients, a senior client should have a thorough medical examination prior to beginning a training regimen.

CARDIOVASCULAR SYSTEM

A senior's body is different than that of a younger adult. Maximum heart rate that a senior can achieve during exercise will lower with advancing age, and overall heart and lung function will also decrease as a person gets older.

This means that a fitness instructor should ease into exercise routines with an older client, using lower weight and workloads to start with and increasing on a very gradual gradient. Training sessions should last from 20 to 45 minutes and should be done three to five times each week. Training intensity should be in the middle range, from 40 to 80 percent.

BODY COMPOSITION

A senior's body composition changes as he or she ages, with lean muscle mass decreasing, bone density lowering and fat stores increasing. In order to help counteract all these factors, weight training is highly recommended to build muscle and decrease fat. Weight-bearing exercise also helps build bone density.

Ideally, the health and fitness professional should start out with lower weights and add more weight on a more gradual gradient. Eight to ten exercises can be chosen, and up to three sets of up to 20 repetitions can be performed to achieve this goal. Training lessons should run for about a half an hour.

NEUROMUSCULAR EFFICIENCY

An older adult will have differences in his or her neuromuscular system that can significantly impact balance, and a fitness instructor needs to be aware of this possibility in order to train the senior safely. Coordination and the person's gait, or way in which they walk, can be impacted as well. Be sure to observe carefully for impairments when performing basic assessments.

In order to deal with any of these issues, the health and fitness professional chooses modes of exercise that are easier for the client. Walking on a treadmill with two handrails, for example, might be a good option, as well as other stationary equipment, such as an exercise bike, or cardiorespiratory training in an aquatic environment.

CARDIAC CONDITION

Older clients may have heart problems that may or may not be diagnosed. Just as with any other client, it is important for an older client to have a full medical exam prior to beginning a workout regimen and get the advice of his or her physician in order to be aware of potential heart complications.

During the health and fitness professional's assessments, it is important to pay special attention to the pulse assessments, noting anything unusual and also determining what base heart rate is normal for this specific client. This will help the trainer know when something is unusual during the course of working with that client.

The normal degeneration that comes with age, along with a lower ability to have a maximum workout, can be challenging for a health and fitness professional in that his or her job is to work against these processes.

Walking is one area that can be especially challenging for seniors, given bone, muscle, coordination, and cardiorespiratory capacity changes. With less ability to move about, a senior is in more danger of having faster degeneration and potentially a greater loss of independence.

Assessment process and intensity level: At the outset of working with a senior client, a health and fitness professional must begin with a series of assessments that will help gauge the client's current exercise capability, physical condition, and overall fitness goals. Begin this process with the Physical Activity Readiness Questionnaire (PAR-Q).

Cardiorespiratory training should be entered into on a gradient, with medications being taken carefully taken into account, as well as other diseases or chronic conditions. Phases 1 and 2 of training will be ideal, with phase 1 being thoroughly explored in order to build up core stability and nervous-system communication to improve balance and coordination before moving on.

COMMUNICATION

When a health and fitness professional works with a senior client, he or she must be aware of potential psychological aspects that may impact the working relationship and approach these with sensitivity and tact.

Senior clients may have fears about engaging in certain types of physical activity. Be sure the client has a thorough physical examination prior to beginning any new workout routine and speaks with his or her doctor about concerns of legitimate physical limitations.

A senior client might be resistant to incorporating weight training into their workout routine because he or she is afraid of injury. Treat this concern with respect, and offer some insight into research showing that resistance training is highly beneficial for seniors.

FLEXIBILITY TRAINING

Flexibility training is important for all clients in order to warm up and cool down muscles, improve range of motion, and add elasticity to connective tissue to reduce risk of injury. Flexibility training is especially important for senior clients who may have lower muscle tone, lower elasticity of body tissues, and lower coordination as a result of aging. Increased flexibility is a good foundation for better training results and ultimately more ability to perform daily activities necessary for independence.

The senior population can benefit greatly from both static stretches and self-myofascial release, while dynamic stretching should be used for warming up and cooling down before and after a workout.

TRAINING MODES

Seniors can engage in cardiorespiratory and weight-training activities, though the trainer should use extra caution for those seniors with balance or coordination problems. For those seniors, equipment with handrails or exercise bikes may be a good choice, as well as aquatic activities. Seniors should work out two to five times each week for up to an hour each day, depending on their ability. The regular set of movement assessments will help the trainer understand these capabilities prior to beginning a workout regimen. All forms of stretching can be considered, depending on the client's ability.

Up to three sets of 8 to 10 different exercises can be employed, using up to 20 repetitions with a lighter weight to begin. Stabilization of the core muscles and overall balance and coordination should factor heavily in the decision of whether to advance.

OBESITY

Obesity is a clinical term defined as the class of people who have a body mass index (BMI) of 30 or greater. BMI is calculated by taking a person's metric weight (in kilograms) and dividing it by their metric height (in meters) squared. Morbid obesity is generally considered to be a BMI greater than 40.

A BMI reading less than 18.5 is considered to be underweight, while a reading of somewhere between 18.5 and 24.9 is considered to be in the healthy range. Clients having BMI readings between 25 and 30 are classified as overweight.

Obese individuals are usually seeking health and fitness training not only for weight loss but also because their overall health status dictates a more healthful lifestyle. Obesity can cause a long list of physical problems that can be addressed in part through regular exercise and a healthy diet.

CAUSES OF OBESITY

Obesity can be caused by a number of individual factors or two or more factors compounding. A main problem, particularly in the United States, is improper energy balance. Simply stated, this means that a person ingests or consumes more calories than he or she burns through activity on a daily basis.

Improper energy balance can occur in two ways: A person may eat an unbalanced, high-calorie diet, or he or she may have a nonactive lifestyle, or both. Given the fast-food culture of the United States and the prevalence of office jobs, in which sitting all day is the norm, it is not surprising that overweight and obesity have been steadily on the rise over the past few generations. Recreational activity is often sedentary: TV watching and video game playing are more common than is playing outside.

AGING

Age can contribute to obesity. As a person ages, the body's lean muscle mass (which burns calories) decreases. Body fat may increase at the same time. Additionally, cardiorespiratory capabilities may decrease along with bone density.

A senior may be less likely to work out regularly because of these degenerative limitations, which can potentially lead into a cycle resulting in the person being overweight or obese. While obesity is not directly correlated with age, the physical problems that come along with aging can result in less physical activity, which in turn leads to the overweight condition.

A health and fitness trainer must take both the person's age and weight into account when beginning a training regimen. The common chronic diseases associated with older age must be factored in, and goals must be set to reduce fat and increase lean muscle mass.

CLIENT'S GAIT

When working with an obese client, the health and fitness professional should be aware that the person's gait, or how the core musculature coordinates the lower part of the body when walking, can be significantly different than a person in the healthy BMI range. This can have a serious impact on balance and coordination.

Research has shown that obese individuals take shorter strides and have lower overall balance, even when they have superior strength. This means that a fitness instructor should focus on coordination first. Stabilization exercises can help maximize core stability while increasing the communication between the brain and nervous system, improving overall coordination.

WEIGHT LOSS

A two-pronged approach should be taken to help an obese client lose weight. This includes both modifying the client's diet and incorporating a systematic exercise regimen.

The client should discuss his or her diet issues with a licensed dietitian. The dietitian will determine a healthful menu or plan for the specific individual, which takes into account overall activity level and constraints from work or family obligations. Support the client's efforts, which will likely include reducing his or her caloric intake by a few hundred calories per day.

Give the client a combination of cardiorespiratory training and weight training to help spur weight loss. Cardiorespiratory training helps improve the body's energy-burning capabilities, and additional lean muscle mass helps burn calories as well.

When working with an obese client, it may be more comfortable for the client, and more effective for the overall workout regimen, for him or her to perform exercises in an upright or recumbent (standing or sitting) position. Machines with cables, as well as isometric exercises that use the person's own body weight may be ideal for a beginning client in this population.

Modification of certain fitness assessments may be advisable as well. Keep all assessments on a manageable gradient in order to get a good idea of fitness capability, but also keep the client safe. For example, squats may be modified to simple balancing, with attention being paid to kinetic-chain compensations that occur while standing on one leg.

Upright stretching may be more comfortable for obese clients. When a floor stretch can be modified into a standing or sitting stretch, try this first.

CORE TRAINING AND STABILIZATION EXERCISES

Because obese individuals often have issues with gait and coordination, stabilization exercises, particularly those that focus on the core musculature, are an excellent starting point for the health and fitness professional.

When working with an obese client, it may be advisable to avoid positions in which the client is reclining or positioned on his or her back due to the higher risk of hypertension found in this population. It may also be more comfortable for an obese client to begin working from standing or seated positions. For example, abdominal work might be easier to begin on a reclining bench rather than on the floor, or by using cables in an upright position.

PSYCHOLOGICAL ASPECTS

When working with someone who is overweight or obese, it is important for the health and fitness professional to be aware of, and sensitive to, the fact that this condition can often cause intense emotional issues for the client. These issues are real and must be dealt with professionally and with tact in order to help the client achieve their ultimate goals.

A fitness instructor must do his or her best to motivate all clients and help them feel as though they are in a safe environment, both for their physical health and for their emotional well-being. This is essential to create a professional relationship founded on trust and cooperation.

Using language that is neutral as to weight, and being thoughtful about encouraging statements, can be very important. Carefully choose your words in order to establish rapport with the client that motivates and keeps the client interested in the training routine, not self-consciously distracted.

COMORBIDITIES

Individuals who are obese are much more likely than persons in the healthy BMI range to have one, if not more, serious health problems that must be taken into account when training. These problems can be a cause of the obesity, or they can be caused by the obesity, but in either event they potentially put the client into more than one special population.

Some common problems obese individuals may have include:

- Diabetes
- Arthritis
- Hypertension
- Asthma

Having the client get a full physical examination prior to beginning a new training routine is essential. This will help spot physical problems and hopefully begin any necessary medical treatment for those problems. Fitness assessments will also help tailor the program to the specific client's capabilities by giving the trainer a view as to kinetic-chain problems, gait problems, and/or musculature compensations.

CARDIOVASCULAR ABILITIES

An obese client may have much different cardiovascular and cardiorespiratory capabilities than a person in the healthy BMI range. The maximum of oxygen that can be taken in during exercise may not be adequate to support his or her body for vigorous activities, and the ability to perform extended, anaerobic workout activities may be limited.

When beginning a workout regimen, include modalities that account for these factors. Often, beginning in an aquatic environment is very helpful. Being submerged in water has many benefits, improving overall condition while avoiding initial overstress on the body and joints. As the client's capabilities improve, walking on flat terrain or on a treadmill might be a good choice to improve cardiovascular endurance and lung capacity.

DIET PROGRAM

Obese clients are much more likely than those in the healthy BMI range to have spent a good deal of their adult lives dieting. This can lead to many hang-ups or misconceptions about diet and exercise that the health and fitness professional must navigate in order to help the client achieve his or her goals.

Be sure the obese client meets with a registered dietitian or nutritionist in order to create a healthy eating plan that reduces daily calories. Low-impact exercise should be the starting point to increase daily activity level, increasing the length of each exercise session to around an hour before increasing the impact level. Calories burned throughout the week should be just over 1,200 to begin with, working up to around 2,000.

BODY COMPOSITION

When working with an obese client, it is best to use BMI as the method of measuring body fat composition. Circumference measurements may also work well. Other methods of body composition measurement may not be accurate for a person who is clinically obese, and taking measurements with skinfold calipers may not appeal to an obese client who is already self-conscious about his or her weight.

The exact measurement of body fat is less important when working with an obese client. BMI measurement is not 100 percent accurate. However, it gives an excellent starting point for the client to use, and it can be used in setting goals for that client because it is a concrete number that can be easily compared to previous measurements.

MODES OF TRAINING

Low-intensity activities may prove ideal when beginning to train with an obese client, such as walking, using a stationary bike, or training in an aquatic environment. Frequency and length of exercise are more important when beginning than is intensity level. Workouts should occur up to five times a week, starting at 20 minutes or so and working up to a full hour before adding more-intense exercises. Workouts can also be done over the course of the day instead of in one sitting: Two 20-minute walks are just as productive as one 40-minute walk if the proper heart rate is reached for both.

Movement assessments should be given to assess client capability, but some squatting exercises can be modified to simple balance exercises if necessary. Observe the kinetic-chain checkpoints for postural distortions.

Up to three sets of 15 repetitions of up to 10 exercises can be performed.

OTHER ISSUES

Obesity is a very significant problem in modern American society, with record numbers of obese children and adults in the United States. Many obese people want to begin a training regimen not only to lose weight but also to alleviate other physical problems that can be exacerbated by being overweight and to improve their overall health and quality of life.

By understanding the common problems associated with this special population, a health and fitness professional can offer superior services to its members. It is important for a fitness instructor to understand not only the additional physical considerations but also the emotional concerns an obese person may have in dealing with a training regimen so the trainer can help guide the client with professionalism and sensitivity.

Reducing calorie intake, increasing activity, and building muscle are the cornerstones of working with an obese client.

DIABETIC INDIVIDUALS

Diabetes describes two related endocrine, or hormonal, disorders. One stems from the inability of the pancreas to produce insulin, a necessary hormone, while the other makes it difficult for the body to convert simple carbohydrates.

More than five percent of the American population has diabetes, and hundreds of thousands of people are newly diagnosed every year. Diabetes affects both young and old persons, and it is a leading cause of death.

A fitness instructor must be aware that a client with diabetes has limitations on his or her body's ability to process, convert, and/or utilize glucose, or blood sugar. While exercise can be very beneficial for a diabetic client, he or she must be monitored carefully to ensure that exercise regimens are safe and that the feet, a common area of injury that is resistant to healing for a diabetic, are protected as much as possible.

TYPE 1 DIABETES

Type 1 diabetes is characterized by an inability of the pancreas to produce the hormone insulin. Because insulin is not circulating in the bloodstream, the cells of the body are not able to convert blood sugar into energy. This creates too much blood sugar (hyperglycemia) and not enough available energy. Type 1 diabetics need to introduce insulin manually into their bodies, usually by injecting synthetic insulin.

This is important because exercise can use blood sugar, so if a diabetic is not mindful of his or her blood sugar levels when engaging in exercise, he or she can use up too much blood sugar, causing levels that are too low (hypoglycemia).

Low blood sugar can cause a person to faint or feel lightheaded. Discuss this potential problem with your client, and ascertain what his or her doctor has recommended as the proper way to deal with it. The client may keep a high-sugar snack or drink on hand for low-blood-sugar incidents.

TYPE 2 DIABETES

Type 2 diabetes is also known as adult-onset diabetes. People who are overweight and eat a diet high in refined foods, especially sugars, can be at a higher risk for developing this type of diabetes. Now more than ever, young people are at a higher risk for developing type 2 diabetes because of poor diet and a higher incidence of overweight.

Type 2 diabetics do not usually have trouble making insulin, which is the primary problem of type I diabetics. Rather, the body cannot properly recognize the insulin and allow it to perform its function of converting blood sugar into a form of energy that cells can readily use.

This means that the blood sugar levels can remain high (hyperglycemia). If the blood sugar remains high over a long period of time, this can cause damage to other parts of the body.

Exercise can help use blood sugar and alleviate some of the stress placed on the body by extra weight.

EXERCISE SELECTION

When working with someone from the special population of diabetics, it is very important for the health and fitness professional to be aware of the client's method of controlling glucose levels. Exercise itself is a very effective method of helping use blood sugar, thus reducing the level of glucose in the bloodstream.

In order to help keep blood glucose levels under control (neither too high nor too low) during exercise, the trainer must have an action plan for the client. This will include knowing when not to train, if the client's body is not ready. The action plan should take into account all recommendations from the client's physician.

It is also important to help the client avoid damage to the feet, such as blisters, infections, or cuts, as they are a sensitive area of the body for diabetics.

COMORBIDITIES

People with diabetes are highly likely to have other conditions that place them in other special populations. This can include being overweight or obese, or being hypertensive (having high blood pressure), among many other problems. It is very important to make sure the diabetic client has a full physical examination before beginning training, so the client's physician can properly diagnose and treat any problems.

Because obesity can be a risk factor of diabetes, as well as a result of diabetes, putting a diabetic client on a training regimen that encourages weight loss and the building of lean muscle tissue is advised. Set the routine to burn at least 1,000 calories each week, working up to 2,000 calories.

GLUCOSE CONTROL MECHANISMS

A person that has diabetes does not have the same glucose control mechanisms that a nondiabetic has. Introducing exercise, which uses blood sugar, into a diabetic's routine must be done with caution. Though exercise is very beneficial to a diabetic in the larger scheme, each training session runs the risk of causing hypoglycemia, or low blood sugar.

Because of this, it is important for the trainer to be able to notice when a client's blood sugar may be dropping. Symptoms of low blood sugar can include fatigue, dizziness, and disorientation. Be sure to have an action plan set up with the client in case this happens.

A client should also be aware that his or her blood sugar can dip many hours after a training session. A person who has had diabetes for some time will likely know how to regulate his or her blood sugar, but a person who is newly diagnosed may want to take more frequent blood sugar readings when starting a training regimen.

BETA BLOCKER MEDICATION USE

Clients who are in the diabetic population often have comorbidities, or other concurrent health problems. A common comorbidity is high blood pressure, or hypertension. Beta blockers are a common medication used to treat this problem.

However, beta blockers can mask the symptoms of dropping blood sugar that may occur during a workout. If the client is not aware of this dip in blood sugar, he or she may develop hypoglycemia, or low blood sugar, during the training session.

To compensate, it may be advisable for the client to take a little less insulin prior to working out, and have simple carbohydrates on hand (juice, snack bar) to ingest before and even during the workout, to keep blood sugar levels under control. If a diabetic client also takes beta blockers, have him or her discuss this with a physician.

TOLERANCE TO HEAT

When a diabetic individual exercises in a hot environment, or when his or her body gets overheated, he or she may not be able to recognize the symptoms of low blood sugar, or hypoglycemia. These symptoms can include fatigue, dizziness, and disorientation.

In order to combat this problem, a health and fitness professional should start training with lower-impact activities, working up to longer training sessions (up to an hour at a time) and more frequent training sessions (up to every day of the week). Exercising daily, or nearly daily, will help control glucose levels. Intensity level should be kept moderate to begin with, giving the client time to acclimate to the workouts and learn to recognize symptoms of hypoglycemia that may occur during training sessions.

TRAINING MODES

In many ways, the guidelines for working with a diabetic client are similar to those for working with an obese individual. The primary difference is in the recommended modality of exercise. While obese clients can greatly benefit from walking as the primary starting point for workouts, this may not be advisable for diabetic clients, whose feet can be susceptible to injuries that do not heal properly. Thus, other exercises, such as aquatic workouts, might be a good starting point.

The basic flexibility continuum can be used, with modifications for self-myofascial release if the client has nervous-system concerns with their feet. Check with the client's physician before recommending self-myofascial release.

TRAINING LENGTH AND INTENSITY

Diabetic clients often have the goals of controlling glucose levels and losing weight. In order to accomplish these goals safely, low-intensity activities (such as riding a stationary bike or performing aquatic exercises) should be employed on a gradual level. Have the client start with short sessions, working up to hour-long sessions, exercising up to seven days a week.

The normal set of assessments will be used, unless there is comorbidity, such as obesity, that should be taken into account. The flexibility continuum can likewise be used.

Two or three resistance-training sessions per week are beneficial. High-level power training is usually not advisable.

Keep all physician recommendations in mind when working with a diabetic client, know the symptoms of hypoglycemia, have a simple carbohydrate source on hand, and be sure the client wears appropriate protective footwear.

HYPERTENSIVE INDIVIDUALS

A person who has hypertension has high blood pressure. This is defined as both the systolic and diastolic readings being too high: The top number (systolic) is greater than 140, and the lower number (diastolic) is more than 90. The reading that should be considered is the one taken when the individual is not taking any medication.

People who smoke, are overweight, or have a high-calorie, high-fat diet are at a higher risk for hypertension. Many of those who have been diagnosed as hypertensive will be on medication to help control the problem, and they may seek exercise as another way to control the hypertension and alleviate some of the underlying causes.

It is important for the health and fitness professional to encourage hypertensive individuals to take the medication prescribed by their doctors. Often, people in this population avoid consistently taking their medications because they do not feel infirm.

BODY POSITIONING

Much like when training overweight, obese, or diabetic clients, improper body position can exacerbate the high blood pressure situation. Positions in which the head is lower than the heart can cause the blood pressure to rise. This may include lying down on the back or on the stomach.

Try to keep the hypertensive client in seated or upright positions for all exercises. To perform abdominal work, the health and fitness professional should consider using cable machines or putting the client on an inclined weight bench.

The trainer should also make sure that the client doesn't overstrain or grip equipment too tightly, as this can also increase blood pressure.

High-intensity power training should be carefully monitored.

BLOOD PRESSURE CHANGE DURING EXERCISE

Unlike an average, nonhypertensive adult, a client with high blood pressure may not have a predictable blood pressure response. It may spike, rise slightly, or vary from session to session. It is important to create a low-impact training routine that gradually increases in frequency, intensity, and duration in order to not aggravate this condition.

Beginning with three sessions per week of 20 minutes per session and building up to five to seven sessions per week of up to an hour will help stabilize the body's blood pressure response over time. Adding more exercise will also help if the client has additional weight loss goals.

Blood Pressure Medication Considerations

Even with medication, a client with high blood pressure may not have his or her condition completely under control prior to arriving for an exercise session. In order to compensate, the health and fitness professional can use program design to support the client's specific needs.

For example, circuit training two or three times a week can be a very effective tool for hypertensive clients. The trainer should select eight to ten exercises and have the client perform up to three sets of a medium to high number of repetitions (somewhere between 12 and 20) per set.

Be sure the client does not overgrip the equipment, avoids Valsalva maneuvers (forcing expiration when the airway is closed), and uses steady, even breathing throughout the training session.

Comorbidities

Hypertension is very often a health problem that is associated with other health problems, such as being overweight or obese or having diabetes. This makes it extremely important for the client to have a thorough physical examination prior to beginning any training regimen and for him or her to discuss potential limitations with the physician.

When creating a training regimen for anyone who belongs to more than one special population, the health and fitness professional should take into account all of the special guidelines for each of the special populations.

A hypertensive routine should aim to burn 1,500 calories each week and work up over time to 2,000. This will encourage weight loss and keep cardiovascular gains on target for supporting the hypertensive condition.

Beta Blocker Use

When a hypertensive client utilizes beta blocker medication, this can alter the way the heart responds to training; therefore, a health and fitness professional should not use the guidelines for maximum heart rate because this formula may not work with the readings resulting from the medication. As an alternative, the talk test (which tests the client's ability to maintain a conversation while exercising) should be used.

If the client's blood pressure exceeds 200 on the top (systolic) reading and 115 on the bottom (diastolic) reading, he or she should not engage in exercise at that time. A fitness instructor should be aware of alternate parameters his or her fitness facility may adhere to.

Training Length and Intensity

Use training modalities that keep the client upright, such as walking and stationary bicycling, in order to avoid body positions in which the head is even with or lower than the heart. Start with three training sessions per week up to daily workouts, which can start out at half an hour and increase in duration up to an hour. The normal assessments may be used along with stretching along the flexibility continuum, using upright or seated positioning.

Circuit training is very beneficial for this special population.

Be sure the client does not grip equipment too tightly and that breathing is regular and even during the workout.

CORONARY ARTERY DISEASE (CAD)

Heart disease is one of the leading causes of death in the United States. Up to 18 million Americans have been diagnosed with CAD or other ongoing heart problems. CAD is generally associated with plaque that collects in the arteries, causing the arteries to narrow and thus resulting in less oxygenated blood traveling to the heart, which can eventually lead to damage of the heart muscle and, ultimately, heart attack.

Diets high in LDL (bad) cholesterol, stress, and use of tobacco products can all contribute to plaque accumulation. It is important to determine if the client has heart-related health concerns and to understand the treatment the client's physician has recommended.

> **Review Video: <u>Coronary Artery Disease</u>**
> Visit mometrix.com/academy and enter code: 950720

RESPONSE TO EXERCISE

Because the client with CAD has special heart-related limitations, it is very important that an accurate measure of the upper levels of capability is ascertained in order to keep the client safe while training. This means that health and fitness professional should not use the traditional methods of estimating heart rate maximum, but it should instead be determined by the client's physician.

Determining the proper heart rate maximum is especially important because a client with CAD may not have the usual symptoms of impending heart trouble, such as sharp pains in the chest. The client may either experience these pains as a chronic problem, therefore not noticing serious chest pains, or he or she might be taking medication that masks these symptoms. Therefore, self-monitoring of heart rate is vital.

COMORBIDITIES

Clients who are in the special population of having CAD often have other related health problems, or comorbidities. These can include being overweight or obese, being diabetic, and/or having high blood pressure. These comorbidities make it extremely important for the client to have a thorough physical examination prior to beginning any training regimen and for him or her to discuss potential limitations with the physician.

When creating a training regimen for anyone who belongs to more than one special population, the health and fitness professional should take into account all of the special guidelines for each of the special populations.

PEAK OXYGEN CAPACITY

The maximum amount of oxygen that can be used is compromised for a person with CAD because the heart muscle is not functioning at top capacity; therefore, the health and fitness professional should begin with low-impact workloads with the guidance of the client's physician or heart specialist. Cardiovascular work should stay below the maximum guidelines suggested by the physician.

Opt for short workouts three times a week, approximately 20 minutes to begin with, and gradually work up to five workouts a week, of an hour in duration. Closely observe how the client is tolerating the workload, and follow the client's capabilities. This will help build the client's heart muscle and overall cardiorespiratory conditioning while proceeding with care due to the client's condition and any medications he or she may be using.

CALORIE INTAKE

A person with CAD should have a minimum goal of burning around 1,500 calories per week to start and work up to 2,000 calories burned through workouts each week. Given the client's condition and potential limitations, be sure to progress very gradually and under the advisement of the client's physician to reach these levels.

After the client has been training steadily and has tolerated the regimen without cardiac symptoms or problems for longer than three months, weight training can be introduced into the workout routine. Select up to ten exercises based on the client's goals and capabilities, and have the client perform up to three sets of each exercise. A moderate to high number of repetitions are recommended (somewhere between 10 and 20). Circuit-style training is advisable to maximize the cardiovascular benefits of the routine.

COMORBIDITIES

CAD is often associated with other health problems, such as being overweight or obese or having diabetes. CAD can also be related to having a diet high in saturated fats and cholesterol. This makes it extremely important for the client to have a thorough physical examination prior to beginning any training regimen and for him or her to discuss potential limitations with the physician. The client should also be referred to a dietitian or licensed nutritionist in order to create a healthful and realistic diet plan to help support the training benefits he or she will derive from fitness training.

When creating a training regimen for anyone who belongs to more than one special population, the health and fitness professional should take into account the guidelines for each of the special populations.

PERCEIVED EXERTION SCALE

Clients with CAD will not be able to use age-related guidelines for the top level of heart rate due to the fact that their heart capacity and heart function are lower than the average client's, which means that their heart rate reading will likely also be lower in a given situation, but since this is an unpredictable measure, other methods must be used.

One way to make sure the client does not exceed the heart rate maximum recommended by his or her physician is by using the perceived exertion scale. This is a subjective test that allows the client to gauge his or her exertion level based on physical cues. The original scale was a spectrum beginning with 6 at the low end and 20 at the high end. A 6 was below very, very light exertion, while a 20 was above very, very hard exertion. The modern category-ratio scale has been modified so that it runs from 0 (no exertion at all) through 11 (absolute top-level exertion).

TRAINING LENGTH AND INTENSITY

ACE recommends beginning work on large muscle areas when commencing training with a person with CAD, including exercises that work the legs and the gluteals, such as walking or working out on a stationary bike.

Start slowly, and progress up to longer and more-frequent workouts. Beginning with 20-minute workouts, three times a week is ideal, and then gradually increases to five weekly workouts of an hour each, as needed, to accomplish the client's overall goals. The talk test and the perceived exertion scale for measuring intensity are recommended, using doctor's guidelines to dictate maximum heart rate.

Be sure to include warm-ups and cool-downs for these clients to help the heart prepare for exercise and to relax afterward.

OSTEOPOROSIS

Osteoporosis is the name of a disease typified by a lower level of bone density, leading to brittle bones that are susceptible to breaking. Osteoporosis is a more-common ailment of postmenopausal women, whose bodies may begin to reabsorb bone cells instead of creating new bone cells, a process which can lead to less-dense bone. This leaves extra space between bone cells, making the bones themselves more porous.

There is also a precursor to osteoporosis known as osteopenia, which is marked by a decrease in overall bone density and can ultimately develop into osteoporosis.

Osteoporosis can be very dangerous for older women, who can suffer irreversible injury if a bone is broken in a fall. Commonly broken bones include the hip and the collarbone; many persons never fully recover after such an injury.

> **Review Video: Osteoporosis**
> Visit mometrix.com/academy and enter code: 421205

PREVENTING OSTEOPOROSIS

There are many documented risk factors for developing osteoporosis. The first risk is being a postmenopausal female. Though men can also develop low bone density, the disease is most often a problem associated with older women.

Lower levels of activity have also been associated with a higher risk of developing osteoporosis because bone cells are formed, in large part, from positive stress being placed on the body. This stress, often from weight-bearing exercise, causes the bones to remodel, or add more bone cells, to compensate, resulting in denser bone tissue.

Lifestyle can also play a role in risk factors. Smoking, drinking alcohol, and poor diet can impact whether someone is at a higher risk for developing osteoporosis.

A health and fitness regimen can help address some of these risk factors by adding physical activity and more-healthful lifestyle choices to a client's life.

OSTEOPOROSIS VS. OSTEOPENIA

It is important for the health and fitness professional to know whether the client has osteopenia or osteoporosis in order to determine how intense his or her weight training can and should be.

If a client has osteopenia, he or she may be able to engage in a higher intensity level of weight training, determined by the trainer using a cost-benefit analysis. Higher intensity levels of weight training can help increase bone density, resulting in somewhat less brittle bones, but may actually increase the client's risk of fracture from the activity itself.

Therefore, with older clients or those who are novices at training or have had low levels of activity throughout life, the focus may be not to increase bone density but to encourage balance and coordination in order to avoid falls altogether.

TRAINING LENGTH AND INTENSITY

Since falls are a very dangerous possibility for people with osteoporosis, cardiorespiratory training that prevents falls is vital. Aquatic activities and supported cardiorespiratory training (recumbent bike or a treadmill with railing) are ideal.

Begin slowly, and gradually increase both frequency and duration. Twice-weekly workouts of 20 minutes are a good starting point, working to up to five weekly workouts of up to 60 minutes each. More than one daily workout might also be useful, breaking up the session into shorter chunks of time.

For people with osteoporosis, the core musculature may be affected by weakened bones. It is very important in order to build up muscle strength, coordination, and balance—all of which will help the client to avoid falling and suffering from injuries. Focus on major hinging areas, such as the hips and thighs, and monitor for proper alignment and posture.

ARTHRITIC INDIVIDUALS

Arthritis is a condition that affects the joints, causing chronic pain and inflammation. There are many different types of arthritis; each causes pain in various joints that can seriously affect a person's ability to perform the daily functions of life, exercise, and/or engage in physical activity.

Osteoarthritis is characterized by a wearing down of the cartilage itself, causing the bones to essentially wear on each other. Rheumatoid arthritis is a condition in which the body attacks its own soft tissues, causing pain and stiffness in the joints, especially in the hands and feet. Rheumatoid arthritis is a chronic degenerative disease of the immune system.

It is important for the trainer to monitor how the training regimen impacts the client's arthritic condition in order to tweak intensity and frequency levels in order to avoid aggravating the condition.

OXYGEN CAPACITY

An arthritic client may have a lower oxygen capacity as a side effect of the arthritic condition due to a decrease in physical activity resulting from the chronic pain and loss of mobility associated with arthritic conditions.

In order to compensate, as well as to minimize aggravation to the condition, workouts can be broken up into shorter segments performed throughout the day. Separate sessions on different equipment can help provide adequate daily cardiorespiratory training, while avoiding overstressing any one joint area. Separate sessions are preferable to single high-impact sessions.

Thirty-minute sessions of cumulative training, performed up to five times each week, are ideal.

ABILITY TO EXERCISE

Clients with arthritic conditions may not be able to perform exercise for a lengthy time and may not be able to exercise as consistently as desired due to acute episodes. The trainer should not force the issue—if a client is having excessive pain and does not feel up to exercising, his or her condition should take precedence. Over time, the client may build up stamina and endurance and be able to exercise more frequently and for longer stretches at a time.

Consider avoiding morning workouts with clients that suffer from rheumatoid arthritis, because these individuals often have early morning pain and stiff joints. Also keep in mind that clients may be using various medications to help control their arthritis pain—be sure that the client follows doctor recommendations for medication use, especially prior to training.

COMORBIDITIES

Arthritis is very often a health problem associated with other health problems, such as having osteopenia or osteoporosis. This makes it extremely important for the client to have a thorough physical examination prior to beginning a training regimen and for him or her to discuss potential limitations with the physician.

When creating a training regimen for anyone who belongs to more than one special population, the health and fitness professional should take into account all of the special guidelines for each of the special populations.

Weight training is highly recommended for persons with arthritis, progressing as much as the client's condition allows. Select up to 10 exercises, and work through them up to three times a week. With arthritic clients, the health and fitness professional will want to use a minimal number of repetitions and work up to a moderate number, somewhere around a dozen.

TRAINING LENGTH AND INTENSITY

Supported modalities of exercise that are low impact in nature are best for arthritic clients. These might include aquatic exercise activities or walking on a treadmill with handrails. The health and fitness professional should progress as the client's condition allows, working from three sessions a week up to five. Sessions should be shorter in length, up to a half an hour, and can be broken up into shorter sessions throughout the day. When beginning, five-minute sessions may be required; use the client's pain threshold as a guide.

Resistance training is advised, using a low to moderate number of repetitions (six to a dozen). Avoid heavy weights, and make sure the client does not overgrip equipment.

CANCER

Cancer is the umbrella term for a variety of disorders characterized by mutated body cells that attack and damage the body. Cancer can very often be fatal, even with aggressive treatment, and is one of the top causes of death in the United States.

Currently, treatment for cancer has improved dramatically, along with long-term prognosis. Research has shown that exercise can help maximize the benefits of treatment and keep a person healthy after treatment is over.

It is important for the health and fitness professional to understand that many of the medications used to treat cancer can have harsh side effects that may affect the ability of the client to train. Clients may feel ill, be anemic, and have cardiac problems caused by cancer medicines. Additionally, cancer treatments fall along a much wider spectrum than those for other ailments and, thus, can have much broader effects.

FATIGUE

Not only does cancer wreak havoc on a client's body, attacking vital cells, organs, and body systems but the medications designed to treat it are also harsh. Going through a cycle of medication can leave a client physically and emotionally exhausted, making it difficult to rally for a training session even when the session is part of their treatment routine.

Cardiovascular training should be low impact and at a moderate level of the client's heart rate capacity, three to five times a week. Breaking up the training cycle throughout the day to hit a cumulative level of 30 minutes of exercise might be the best option for a client with cancer. Walking, rowing, and using a stationary bicycle are all good options for clients in this population.

IMMUNE FUNCTION AND MUSCLE TISSUE

Cancer and its various treatments can affect the body in a multitude of different ways. Immune system function will be lower due to the onslaught of medications that are used to kill cancer cells. Exercise can help increase immune function and improve the client's overall condition, adding an emotional boost.

Weight training is especially effective. Select up to 10 appropriate exercises for the client, and have them perform just one set of a low to moderate number of repetitions (around a dozen) a few times per week, as their body allows. This will help combat the diminishment of lean muscle that can result from cancer and its various treatments. Pay special attention to coordination and balance deficiencies that may occur because of the loss of muscle mass.

TRAINING LENGTH AND INTENSITY

Clients with cancer face physical challenges unique to their special population, including physical weakness and acute fatigue that may come and go depending on the day or the stage of their treatment they are in. Shorter sessions throughout the day, lasting 10 to 15 minutes each and adding up to about 30 minutes of cardiorespiratory training, are best to avoid overtaxing the body. Work up to training three to five times per week, as the client is able.

Walking and working on a stationary bicycle are good modalities of exercise.

One set of up to 10 exercises, with low repetitions, is an ideal way to start with weight training.

PREGNANCY

A pregnant woman is a female currently carrying a fetus through a 40-week gestational period. The body of a pregnant woman is undergoing dramatic changes in its efforts to support the growing baby and prepare for birth, causing physiological changes ranging from hormonal shifts, a loosening of ligaments and connective tissue, increased blood volume, and changes in gait and balance.

Exercise has been shown to be extremely beneficial to pregnant women, helping them prepare for the rigors of childbirth and recover once the baby is born. However, it is very important that the health and fitness professional understand the physical changes that women go through in order to keep both mother and child safe.

EXERCISE LIMITATIONS

There are many conditions of pregnancy that will severely limit, if not preclude entirely, any exercise regimen. It is vital that a health and fitness professional know these conditions in order to avoid training a pregnant woman who is experiencing any of them.

If a pregnant woman is experiencing bleeding in the second or third trimesters, she should be examined by her physician prior to proceeding with any exercise. Heavy vaginal bleeding during pregnancy is a serious warning sign that should not be ignored.

Cervical issues, such as early dilation (incompetent cervix) or improper placenta placement, must be addressed by the woman's physician before exercise commences.

High blood pressure during pregnancy can also be a serious problem as well as gestational diabetes, in which pregnancy hormones interfere with the body's ability to properly process and use glucose. While exercise can help with these conditions, it is essential that the pregnant woman consult with her physician first.

BLOOD VOLUME

When a woman is pregnant, her body can produce up to a third more blood volume than she might normally have. This is a protective mechanism that helps support the demands of the growing fetus while ensuring the woman has an extra blood supply should she bleed during delivery.

Despite having more blood volume, a pregnant woman may have a lower oxygen capacity for training sessions. She may also experience shortness of breath if the fetus is situated in such a way as to be pressing upward on her lungs.

To compensate for these factors, lower impact exercises are advised. Aquatic exercises or machine-based cardiorespiratory training are best, avoiding heavy weights. The trainer should begin with three sessions per week and work up to five.

NUTRITIONAL NEEDS

A pregnant woman has higher nutritional demands than other individuals by virtue of literally growing another person. It is generally accepted that a pregnant woman needs an extra 300 calories each day to support the fetus and to build fat stores for breast-feeding once the child is born.

When a woman adds exercise to her activities, she must compensate for this added caloric expenditure. Pregnant women are not advised to diet or engage in weight loss during pregnancy. Additionally, pure calorie intake is not the goal; rather, calories derived from nutritionally sound sources rich in calcium and other vitamins and minerals are needed to support fetal growth.

In order to determine a positive nutritional balance that factors in fitness activities, be sure the client discusses her training routine with her physician and a dietitian or nutritionist, who will give professional advice on the most healthful options for her particular gestational stage.

RISK CATEGORIES

Some women are considered to be at a higher risk of developing serious complications during pregnancy. Major risk factors include age (women older than 35 are considered at higher risk for complications and for having a baby with certain birth defects); history of pregnancy-related problems, such as miscarrying; endocrine problems (thyroid or insulin-related); and being obese or overweight.

These risk factors potentially add more stress onto the already hardworking pregnant body. If the client has risk factors, be sure that she has discussed any training routine with her physician. Weight training should only be engaged in if endorsed by her doctor. Closely observe how the client is tolerating training in order to keep track of notable changes.

LOOSENING OF THE LIGAMENTS

During pregnancy, hormones are released by the woman's body to help prepare for childbirth. These include hormones that loosen ligaments, specifically to help with pelvic joints that must accommodate the baby's head during birth. However, the hormones do not discriminate among ligaments, and there can be a loosening of all connective tissues throughout the body.

Loosened ligaments are very important to be aware of when working with a pregnant woman because she may have less control of her core musculature and balance. She may have dull or sharp pain in the groin and pelvic area from the loosened ligaments. Consider using supported cardiorespiratory training, such as aquatic activities and walking on a treadmill with handrails. Also use extra caution with weight-bearing exercises.

TRAINING LENGTH AND INTENSITY

There are several important things to keep in mind when working with a pregnant client. Due to the added pressure that the fetus places on the circulatory system, avoid exercises that require the client to lie on her back. Also, be sure she does not overheat or overexert because core body temperature tends to run higher for pregnant women.

Lower-intensity activities are ideal for pregnant women. Be sure to avoid activities that require the client to lie on her back because the weight of the baby pressing on the vena cava can cause her to become dizzy or even to pass out. Sessions should range from three to five per week, with weight training incorporated once or twice per week.

POSTPARTUM CONSIDERATIONS

Exercise and fitness training are excellent ways for a postpartum mother to combat fatigue and help her body return to its prepregnancy shape. However, the health and fitness trainer must be aware of certain aspects of postpartum training before commencing with someone who has recently given birth.

Generally, women are discouraged by their physicians from entering into exercise routines for the first six weeks after childbirth. Giving birth is a strenuous task that requires downtime for the body to heal, and the period immediately following birth is one of great transition as a woman adapts to caring for a baby while her hormone levels shift dramatically and she begins breastfeeding, if she is choosing to do so. Complications during the birth, or a surgical delivery, can lengthen recovery time.

Many women are so keen on returning to their prepregnancy weight that they rush to work out before physically advisable. When beginning a training routine with a woman who has just had a baby, be sure her doctor has sanctioned such activity.

Lung Disorders

Lung disease is an umbrella term for any chronic disorder of the pulmonary system. In many instances, it is causes by smoking cigarettes or having been exposed to second-hand smoke.

There are two general types of lung disorders: obstructive disorders and restrictive disorders. Obstructive lung disease is characterized by lower lung function caused by an obstruction, oftentimes the body's own fluids, getting in the way of the free flow of gases. Obstructive lung diseases include emphysema and asthma. In restrictive lung disease, such as pulmonary fibrosis, the actual lung tissue is damaged and does not function properly.

Whichever category the disorder falls into, the result on training is approximately the same: The client has impaired oxygen levels, which result in reduced stamina and increased tiredness and dizziness at low-impact levels.

Physical Characteristic

People who have chronic lung disorders may show the physical signs of the wear the disease places on the body. Those with obstructive lung disease may be underweight and have lower muscle tone. Those with restrictive lung disease may show the effects of constantly working against their bodies to breathe: They may be overweight and have oversized rib cages.

Working with a person who has lung disease, however, is much like working with a regular adult. The health and fitness professional should understand that energy levels and stamina may be lower and adjust accordingly. Additionally, the trainer should focus on lower-body activities to avoid stressing upper-body muscles that may be compensating for pulmonary issues. Adequate rest times need to be incorporated into the workout to help the person catch his or her breath or recover from heightened activity.

Comorbidities

People who are in the special population of those with lung disease often have other physical conditions, or comorbidities, that can also affect a health and fitness training regimen. Often, people with lung disease may be long-term smokers who may also have problems with their hearts (lack of oxygen to the heart muscle over time can cause an enlarged heart and other vascular problems).

This makes it extremely important for a client with a history of lung disease to have a thorough examination with his or her physician prior to commencing physical training, giving the client and the trainer parameters for safely working around the lung disease issues and to diagnose and treat other concurrent health problems.

OXYGEN CONVERSION

One of the primary problems faced by someone with any type of lung disease is a lower level of oxygen being converted for the body's use at any given time. Adding more stress on the cardiovascular system by introducing exercise, even low-impact activities, further taxes the pulmonary system.

The lower oxygen levels can cause shortness of breath even when the client is engaged in very-low-impact activities. A health and fitness professional should be aware of how to use a pulse oximeter to obtain oxygen levels during exercise to ensure they do not dip below acceptable levels. Results are recorded in order to compare them to future readings, to ascertain whether the client is tolerating certain activities well and to determine if improvements in oxygen levels are being made.

PHYSICAL SHAPE

A person with lung disease is more likely to be out of shape than the average healthy adult. Lung disease may limit activities and promote a more-sedentary lifestyle, making the person's cardiovascular health level lower and promoting muscle atrophy.

In order to reverse these limitations, regular exercise will be helpful. Under the guidance and supervision of the client's physician, work your way up to 20 minutes to 45 minutes of exercise up to five times each week. Observe closely how well the client is tolerating the routine, and let his or her comfort level dictate the pace at which you progress. Consider breaking up training sessions throughout the day, so as not to overtax the pulmonary system with one long session. More rest time may be needed to allow recuperation between exercises or sets.

UPPER BODY TRAINING REGIMEN

Training a client with pulmonary considerations may impact the types of exercises you should choose for him or her. Specifically, a health and fitness professional should choose exercises that target lower-body muscle groups or lower-body activity, such as using a stationary bike, and avoid exercises that tax the upper-body muscles.

Clients with lung disorders have alternate muscle group usage, which stems from the fact that the body must work harder to breathe. Alternate muscles may be recruited to help with this process—muscles that are not normally used for breathing. Upper-body workouts can doubly tax these muscle groups, causing general shortness of breath and fatigue much faster than lower-body workouts.

MUSCLE MASS

When a person has a serious pulmonary disorder, it can result in not only muscle loss from lack of exercise but also serious, even severe, atrophy resulting in an unhealthy BMI that is below the healthy range (which begins at 18).

If the client is especially underweight, be sure that he or she is referred to a nutritionist or dietitian in order to create a healthy eating plan that incorporates more calories to make up for those used in training sessions. Incorporate weight training into the routine in order to build muscle mass and to help the client put on weight.

OXYGEN TANK CONSIDERATION

Some clients with lung disorders may need an oxygen tank to keep their oxygen levels within safe parameters, both during exercise and possibly even in daily life. This can present a unique challenge in health and fitness training activities.

It is vitally important for health and fitness professionals to understand that they may not interfere with or adjust the levels of oxygen that a client is taking, as this is a medical treatment that only a physician can administer and control. Use a pulse oximeter to keep track of oxygen saturation levels during exercise, recording your results over all of the client's sessions to keep track of notable patterns. Should the client experience difficulty with oxygen levels, the physician must be consulted.

PULMONARY ISSUES

Low-impact activities are the best for those with impaired lung function, especially those that work the lower extremities and avoid taxing the upper body. Training sessions should be short, starting with 20 minutes and working up to 45 minutes, as much as the client can tolerate. Several shorter sessions in a day may be more attainable than one long session.

Weight training should be kept easy: two or three sessions of only one set of repetitions per exercise a couple of times a week.

Be sure to give the client adequate rest time between sets or exercises; this time might be longer than for the average client.

PERIPHERAL ARTERY DISEASE (PAD)/INTERMITTENT CLAUDICATION

Peripheral artery disease (PAD) is a disorder in which a person's arteries do not function properly due to a narrowing of the arteries or a failure of the artery closure flaps. This results in poor lower-body circulation that can affect training. Intermittent claudication is the umbrella term for the effects of PAD.

One of the main symptoms of PAD is pain in the legs, which can limit a client's ability to train. The health and fitness professional will have to proceed slowly in order to determine whether this pain is due to PAD or is associated with beginning a training regimen. It is important that the client have a full physical examination to beginning the training regimen and that all the doctor's recommendations are followed.

Training sessions should proceed according to the client's tolerance for pain or discomfort. If there is ongoing pain in training sessions, have the client discuss the problem with his or her physician before carrying on.

COMORBIDITIES

Clients with PAD are often prone to having other health problems, or comorbidities. Coronary artery disease is a common problem as well as insulin-related disorders, such as type 1 and type 2 diabetes.

If a client has coronary artery disease in addition to PAD, the health and fitness professional should make sure the client stays within a set heart rate maximum. (This upper limit can be determined using a test in which the client walks to the extent his or her pain will permit.)

Be careful not to just ignore the leg pain and have the client perform a different type of exercise. Leg pain acts as a good upper-level indicator, and it can help prevent overworking the heart.

Walking is the ideal exercise for those with PAD, and it should be engaged in for at least 10-minute sessions.

SMOKING

If a client with PAD smokes, quitting is highly desirable. Have the client discuss methods of quitting with his or her physician, as the effects of smoking on circulation can be exponentially more dangerous when combined with PAD. Smoking also lessens the client's ability to perform the exercise routine.

There are many options for quitting smoking that should be explored, including medications. Tread lightly when discussing this topic with the client because many smokers have indulged for many years and may be resistant to any perceived negative judgments of this habit.

If the client cannot or will not quit, try to get him or her to agree to not smoke for a time period preceding health and fitness workouts, such as 60 minutes or more.

STAMINA

Clients with PAD are more likely to be significantly out of shape when compared to the average healthy adult due to leg pain, which limits their fitness activities. PAD itself can affect a person's ability to circulate oxygenated blood, leading to fatigue more quickly than with the average healthy adult.

Walking is recommended by ACE for people with peripheral artery disease. Walking is well tolerated and can be made more challenging by increasing speed or incline on a treadmill.

If the client is having difficulty with pain, consider breaking up the workout into shorter chunks of time, aiming to have at least 10-minute segments at a time.

WEIGHT TRAINING

Weight training is recommended for members of this special population insofar as resistance training is beneficial to people in general, but it may not have a direct benefit to the PAD problem itself; therefore, cardiorespiratory training should be the main focus of a program for a client who has PAD, with a few supplementary weight training sessions per week.

These sessions should incorporate up to 10 exercises and can include up to three sets of a moderate number of repetitions (around 10). Working in a circuit method maximizes the cardiorespiratory training.

Be sure to allow adequate rest time and to progress to the extent that the client's pain will allow.

TRAINING LENGTH AND INTENSITY

Aerobic exercises, such as walking and using a stationary bicycle, are recommended for clients who have pulmonary issues. Sessions should start with three per week and progress up to five, as the client can tolerate. Sessions should be relatively short, beginning with 20 minutes and topping out at 60 minutes. Consider breaking the session up over the day, aiming for shorter sessions of more than 10 minutes each.

Weight training can be incorporated, but it should be secondary in focus to aerobic exercise. These sessions should incorporate up to 10 exercises and can include up to three sets of a moderate number of repetitions (around 10). Working in a circuit method maximizes the cardiorespiratory training.

EFFECTIVE COMMUNICATION OF PROPER TECHNIQUE AND FEEDBACK

When giving feedback to a client regarding proper technique for exercise, the fitness instructor should utilize as many avenues as possible to communicate. The trainer can verbally explain the proper technique needed. He should follow this with a demonstration of the movement pattern. The client should then attempt the movement pattern one time without any additional weight or resistance of any kind. As the client is performing the movement, the fitness instructor should be spotting her and providing verbal cues the entire time. Throughout the process, the client should be allowed to ask questions and encouraged to do so. When giving feedback regarding client performance, the trainer should begin with what the client has been doing correctly so far and any ways she has improved since the initial exercise testing. Additionally, once the trainer has given feedback to the client, the client should be allowed to ask questions. In areas where the client is still deficient in performance, the trainer should share with her a plan for improvement.

Feedback can be given to a client in a variety of ways. Evaluative feedback helps the client know what she is doing correctly and incorrectly in the movement pattern ("You are doing a great job of not allowing your knees to go past your toes, but make sure your toes are pointed forward."). Supportive feedback is a means of encouraging the client, perhaps through a difficult part of the workout ("I know it's tough, but we're almost through. Do you think you can finish 2 more laps?"). Descriptive feedback is clear and concise feedback that provides correction at the end of a movement pattern or session ("In future squat-type exercises, I want you to focus on squeezing the muscles of your gluteus to decrease pressure on your knees."). Feedback should be given to the client verbally at regular intervals, but also in written form when she is regularly evaluated for goal assessment.

COMMUNICATION WITH CLIENTS

There are various ways of communicating information with a client, and the fitness instructor must find out which types of communication will be most beneficial for the client. Talking with the client over the phone is most beneficial if the client can be reached easily via telephone, although the fitness instructor needs to understand the protocol of the fitness center for making such calls from her personal number. Depending on the fitness facility, email and text reminders for appointments can be appropriate if done through a business email or contact number. The fitness instructor needs to be careful about sending personal information regarding the client through these avenues. Additionally, keeping an updated newsletter or website can be a means of communicating mass information to several clients; however, some clients may not use these sources as a general rule.

VERBAL AND NONVERBAL COMMUNICATION

Communication throughout the exercise session is both verbal and nonverbal. The fitness instructor should give verbal instructions and encouragement to the client while also realizing that her body language will impact the client as well. It is important to make eye contact with the client and speak kindly and confidently to him so he understands that his fitness instructor views his time and effort as important. The fitness instructor should maintain a professional appearance at all times, maintaining a pleasant facial expression and keeping her attention focused on the client throughout the session.

ACTIVE LISTENING

Active listening means that the fitness instructor is listening to what the client has to say, looking at the client while she speaks, and asking questions at appropriate times to be sure of what the client means. Examples of active listening would be making eye contact with the client, jotting down notes regarding what the client is saying, ensuring he understands the client's request ("So what I understand you to mean is..."), and making any necessary changes to the workout routine based on the client's feedback.

STRATIFYING CLIENT RISK AND OBTAINING MEDICAL CLEARANCE TO MINIMIZE NEGLIGENCE

Negligence is defined as the breach of the duty of care between a professional and a client. If a fitness instructor doesn't take time to stratify client risk and obtain medical clearance if indicated, she will be seen as negligent should anything happen to the client during the course of exercise programming. The fitness instructor is obligated to do everything in her power to ensure the client is exercising in a safe environment with minimal risk to health and well-being; stratifying client risk and obtaining medical clearance meets this professional requirement.

LEVELS OF RISK STRATIFICATION

The Health History Questionnaire enables clients to see specifically which risk factors affect them. For instance, the following risk factors could indicate coronary artery disease: hypertension, family history, high cholesterol, cigarette smoking, impaired fasting glucose, obesity, sedentary lifestyle. Additionally, risk factors can also be assessed during the exercise session. The following risk factors could indicate pulmonary, metabolic, or cardiovascular disease: pain or tension in chest, neck, jaws, arms, or other areas; dizziness; shortness of breath; orthopnea or nightly dyspnea; palpitations; ankle edema; known heart murmur; intermittent claudication; unusual fatigue or shortness of breath during normal activities. Clients can be stratified as low, moderate, or high risk based upon the aforementioned symptoms.

HYDRATION

Hydration plays an important role in exercise; it allows the cardiovascular system to function properly, keeps internal temperature at acceptable levels, and allows the body to perspire and cool itself effectively. If a client is dehydrated prior to exercise, the heart rate may increase too quickly to unsafe levels, and she will tire more easily with less effort. If a client doesn't replace the water lost through effort and perspiration following an exercise session, she can also dehydrate which will put excess strain on the cardiovascular system.

PROPER NUTRITIONAL AND PORTION GUIDANCE

If a client is seeking help about establishing better nutritional habits and portion control, the fitness instructor should be ready to provide resources. Some resources include ACE dietary guidelines as found on their website, www.myplate.gov, and websites where clients can gain access to guidance on healthy meals they can make. Additionally, if a client eats out frequently, the fitness instructor can show him how to navigate a restaurant website to find the healthiest option and how to have a backup plan for unexpected times of eating out.

Professional Responsibility

STANDARD OF CARE

The standard of care is the minimum criteria of behavior for a responsible professional. For a fitness instructor, adhering to the standard of care means providing all the services which a reasonable person of ordinary prudence would expect for a fitness instructor to provide. If the fitness instructor is found to have failed to meet the standard of care, he or she may be considered negligent. Insofar as he or she is acting as a professional, a fitness instructor bears all the responsibilities of care and for the participants in his or her exercise class. The general characteristics of the standard of care are determined both by the ACE code of ethics and any relevant state, federal, and local laws.

NEGLIGENCE

Negligence can be defined as any failure to meet the standard of care. For a fitness professional, negligence is the failure to perform the duties and bear the responsibilities outlined by the ACE and the government. Acts of negligence are distinguished from other violations by being unintentional. Although the behavior of the negligent individual may be wanton or reckless, it should not be intentionally injurious of another person. In making a ruling on a question of negligence, the court will try to decide whether a reasonable person would consider the behavior of the fitness instructor to be negligent.

In the case of contributory negligence, the court acknowledges that the injured party may have in some way, and possibly unwittingly, contributed to their own injury. Oftentimes, the individual who is accused of professional negligence will allege that the victim has contributed to his or her own injury. Another scenario in which degrees of negligence may be debated is known as comparative negligence. In the case of comparative negligence, both parties involved bear some responsibility for the injury, and the mission of the court is to determine each party's contribution.

ASSUMPTION OF RISK

In many cases, an individual who is accused of negligence will try to prove that the plaintiff had made an assumption of risk. In other words, the defendant will attempt to show that the plaintiff was aware of the dangers involved in the activity during which the plaintiff was injured. For example, a fitness instructor who is accused of negligence after a participant is injured during a kickboxing routine might attempt to prove to the court that the participants had been briefed on the dangers of the routine before its initiation. If the defendant can prove that the plaintiff was aware of the risks, the defendant may be able to avoid being convicted of negligence, so long as his or her own conduct was not especially irresponsible.

Fitness instructors use two different kinds of documents to establish the participants' assumption of risk and guard against charges of negligence. The first of these, the waiver, is the voluntary abandonment or surrender of the legal right to

92

act. An individual who signs a waiver declares that he or she is aware of the risks involved in the proposed activity, and will not hold the instructor liable for any injuries that occur. An informed consent form, meanwhile, establishes that the participant has been briefed on the possible risks of the proposed activity, and has decided to participate anyway. By signing an informed consent, the participants only agrees to those practices that are explicitly mentioned in the document.

SCREENING AND TESTING LIABILITIES

At the initiation of an exercise program, it is in the best interests of the fitness instructor to collect as much information as possible about each participant. To this end, the fitness instructor should have each participant fill out a basic health screen document. The information contained in this document should be treated with the utmost confidentiality. Furthermore, once the document is completed, the fitness instructor is responsible for creating a fitness program that takes into account all the information listed in the document. If a fitness instructor is found to have designed a fitness program that violates specific medical requirements listed in the health screen document, the fitness instructor may be held liable in a court of law.

ACCURATE INFORMATION

The content of an exercise class must always be intellectually accurate and in conformance with the recognized standards of the profession. An instructor who encourages the participants in the class to perform dangerous or improper exercise routines may be held liable by the participants for any resulting injury. A failure to achieve the basic knowledge required of a fitness instructor can be construed by the court as criminal negligence. Furthermore, fitness instructors should only provide those services for which they have been specifically trained. For example, a fitness instructor should not provide first aid or any other emergency service unless he or she has been specifically certified to provide that service.

SUPERVISION LIABILITY

One of the basic components of the professional standard of care for a fitness instructor is to provide adequate supervision during the performance of complex and potentially injurious exercise routines. Not only is a fitness instructor charged with monitoring the students in the class during the course of the exercise routine, but he or she is responsible for ensuring that participants do not attempt exercise routines that are beyond their physical abilities. In order to effectively monitor an exercise class, a fitness instructor should take care to make sure the class size is not too large. The more complex and potentially dangerous the activity, the fewer students should be in the class.

FACILITY LIABILITY

Part of a fitness instructor's professional standard of care is maintaining safe and effective exercise facilities. In a safe exercise facility, there will be enough room for all participants, and the instructor will have a vantage point from which to monitor the performance of the participants. The floor surface must be adequate, with no loose fringe in the carpet or wet spots on the hardwood or cement. All the

93

equipment that is to be used during the exercise program should be clean and safe. A fitness instructor can be held liable for any failure to provide safe and adequate facilities to the participants in the exercise program. When problems arise, it is the responsibility of the fitness instructor to alert participants to these problems and then seek to mitigate them as soon as possible.

EQUIPMENT LIABILITY

A fitness instructor can be liable for any defects in the fitness equipment that lead to injury by the participants. In order to make sure that all fitness equipment conforms to the current standards, a fitness instructor will have to stay abreast of the professional literature concerning fitness equipment. Broken equipment should be removed from the class environment immediately. Equipment that is potentially dangerous should be inspected before every class session. Whenever significant wear and tear develops on a piece of equipment, the instructor should take that piece of equipment out of circulation until it can be determined whether or not it poses a danger to the participants in the class. In all situations regarding faulty equipment, a fitness instructor should err on the side of caution.

COPYRIGHTS

There is more information available on the subjects of fitness and exercise science today than there has been at any other point in history. However, much of this information is copyrighted and protected by intellectual property rights law, meaning that it cannot be used by a fitness instructor without receiving explicit permission from the creator. Whenever borrowing directly from another source, a fitness instructor should obtain permission from the copyright owner. Also, the music used during a fitness class must be paid for. Typically, an exercise facility will purchase a comprehensive license that allows them to use all music during their exercise programs. In some situations, however, it may be necessary for an instructor to purchase an individual license.

In order to protect one's rights as a creator of intellectual content, one must obtain a copyright. This issue is especially pertinent for fitness instructors, who often develop their own personal routines and music for the use in exercise classes. In order to prevent this material from being pirated by other fitness instructors, the creator must obtain a copyright through the United States Copyright Office. Only certain types of work may be copyrighted. For instance, a piece of choreography must be fairly long in order to receive copyright consideration from the federal government. Any printed media, as for instance books, videos, or films, will typically be copyrighted as part of the publishing process.

SCOPE OF PRACTICE

The scope of practice is the range of activities, procedures, and responsibilities that are granted to an individual holding a certain certification. Certified fitness instructors, therefore, have a specific set of activities and responsibilities that they are certified to provide and bear. A fitness instructor is not allowed to provide advice or service in any area in which he or she has not been specifically trained and licensed. In other words, a fitness instructor is not allowed to provide medical advice to participants. It is proper for a fitness instructor to refer participants to another professional who is trained in the area of concern. Fitness instructors who wander beyond the appropriate scope of practice may be held liable by a court.

INDEPENDENT CONTRACTOR VERSUS EMPLOYEE

An independent contractor is a person who agrees to do a certain piece of work according to his or her own preferences. The relationship between an independent contractor and his or her employer is typically more flexible than that between an employee and employer. In most cases, the independent contractor is given the freedom to accomplish his or her objectives in whatever manner he or she sees fit. An employee, on the other hand, is likely to be under constant supervision by the employer. Employers are not required to pay Social Security or Medicare taxes on behalf of an independent contractor. The relationship between an independent contractor and employer may be terminated after the fulfillment of the contract by either party.

CONTRACTS

Many fitness instructors work as independent contractors, meaning that they agree with their employer to provide specific services without explicitly defining the manner in which those services will be provided. In most cases, the instructor will be required to sign a legal contract specifying the services that he or she has agreed to provide. In order to be considered a valid contract, there must be an offer, an acceptance of the offer, an explanation of the payment to be rendered, and an explanation of any other terms within which the work must be performed. Also, all those who sign the contract should be legally capable of doing so. In order to protect his or her rights as an independent contractor, a fitness instructor should study the terms of the contract.

AMERICANS WITH DISABILITIES ACT

According to the Americans with Disabilities Act, individuals must be given access to services regardless of their physical ability. In the context of fitness instruction, this means that no exercise facility can deny the right to participate in exercise programs to disabled individuals. Exercise programs are required to have easy access for disabled individuals, as well as equipment that can be used by individuals in all forms of disability. Whenever possible, fitness instructors should make appropriate adjustments for the disabled individuals in the exercise program. Any fitness instructor or exercise facility may be held liable for the failure to provide adequate services for the disabled.

FITNESS ENVIRONMENT RISKS

A certain amount of risk is inevitable during the course of an exercise program. There are a few different ways that a fitness instructor can try to diminish the chance of injury. One way is by eliminating all the activities that present an especially high level of risk. Another way to minimize risk is to regularly update and maintain the exercise facilities and equipment. Fitness facilities may also wish to minimize risk by purchasing insurance. Many businesses find that it is more prudent to pay a small, regular sum to offset the risk of injuries than to be surprised by a catastrophic accident.

INSURANCE

There are a few different kinds of insurance that fitness instructors may wish to purchase in order to offset risk. Professional liability insurance protects the fitness instructor against potential claims of negligence. Disability insurance protects the instructor in case he or she becomes seriously ill or injured. Individual medical insurance will help pay for hospitalization and other medical treatment in the event of serious illness or injury. General liability insurance will help pay for medical care in the event of basic injuries suffered by participants in an exercise program.

ACCIDENT REPORTS

Whenever an accident occurs during an exercise class or at an exercise facility, a detailed accident report should be completed immediately after the injured party has been assisted. The accident report should contain the following information: a detailed description of the injury; the equipment involved; the employees or independent contractors present at the time of the accident; a list of witnesses; the personal data of the injured party; and the signatures of all involved parties. Accident report should be kept on file for as long as the statute of limitations dictates.

AMERICAN COUNCIL ON EXERCISE

The primary focus of all fitness instructors must be on providing safe and effective instruction. This means that a fitness instructor must cultivate the ability to ignore any potential distractions to his or her mission. Fitness instructors who work in a large exercise facility too often become enmeshed in organizational politics, and lose sight of their primary objective. The American Council on Exercise requires that every fitness instructor perform the necessary duties to make sure that a fitness class is challenging and safe for all the participants.

In their professional lives, fitness instructors are likely to come into contact with individuals representing the entire spectrum of physical ability. To be effective, a fitness instructor needs to learn to deal with individuals of varying abilities fairly. On occasion, fitness instructors become too preoccupied with the low functioning members of the class, and neglect those members who are more capable of self-monitoring. In other classes, the instructor focuses too closely on fine tuning the more advanced members of the class, and alienates beginners. At all times, a fitness instructor needs to make sure that he or she is including all the members of the class, and responding to each of their individual fitness needs.

Part of being a professional fitness instructor is keeping abreast of the latest health and fitness research, and bringing this information to class. There are numerous fitness journals and magazines, including some published by the federal government, that contain helpful research and guidelines for fitness instructors. In addition, a great deal of medical research has direct application for fitness instructors. Whenever a member of the fitness class has questions about a particular area of fitness knowledge, the instructor should be able to quickly find the appropriate information.

In order to be prepared in the event of an emergency during an exercise class, each fitness instructor should acquire and maintain cardiopulmonary resuscitation certification and should be skilled in the administration of other first-aid services. The American Red Cross offers frequent certification classes, all of which are appropriate for fitness instructors. A fitness instructor should always know the location of the first-aid kit in the exercise facility, and should be familiar with the procedure for contacting emergency services. It is a good idea to practice emergency situations once or twice a year, so that there is no confusion when an actual emergency arises.

In their professional lives, fitness instructors are required to abide by all appropriate business, employment, and intellectual property laws. It is unlawful for fitness instructors to discriminate by age, gender, race, religion, or ethnicity when making hiring decisions. As for intellectual property laws, it is improper for a fitness instructor to use the work of a published author without express consent. There are a number of copyrighted physical fitness programs on the market; fitness instructors should always obtain permission to borrow content from these programs before doing so.

In order to be effective as a fitness instructor one must obtain as much information about the participants in the class as possible. This information, however, will often be personal and should be granted the highest degree of confidentiality. In other words, personal information about the participants in an exercise class should not be disclosed unless the safety of the individual or other members of the class is in danger. Any information that is gathered and shared for research purposes should only be done so with the express consent of the individual in question. Only the fitness instructor should have access to the documentation used during the creation of a fitness profile at the beginning of an exercise program.

Occasionally, one of the participants in a fitness program will have questions or needs that cannot be met by the class instructor. In such cases, the instructor is obliged to refer the participant to a more qualified health or medical professional. Under no circumstances should a fitness instructor provide advice or guidance on the subject in which he or she has not been trained. Of course, the fitness instructor must obtain permission from the client before sharing any information about the client with another professional. In all cases, the fitness instructor should place the well-being of the client ahead of his or her own professional advancement.

Every fitness instructor is an ambassador for the entire health and fitness industry. As such, he or she must strive to maintain a positive relationship with the community. This positive relationship begins in the exercise class environment, as the fitness instructor continually strives to maintain a good rapport with all students. Outside of class, however, a fitness instructor should also endeavor to promote healthy lifestyles. Ideally, a fitness instructor's life will be a living example for the community. Whenever possible, the fitness instructor should seek to promote the interests of the health and fitness industry.

In order to be effective, a fitness instructor will need to build close relationships with his or her clients. However, a fitness instructor should always take care to keep relationships professional. It is inappropriate for a fitness instructor to become romantically involved with a student in his or her class. If an instructor feels that a member of the class is developing inappropriate feelings for him or her, the instructor should immediately confront the student and resolve the issues.

EMERGENCY PROCEDURES

When an emergency situation occurs during a fitness class, time is of the essence. It is for this reason that fitness instructors should be certified in cardiopulmonary resuscitation and first aid. While other students in the class contact emergency services, a fitness instructor needs to be ready to provide immediate care to the injured party. In any situation where the participant has stopped breathing, a fitness instructor should begin CPR. If the individual is clearly suffering a heart attack, a fitness instructor should use the exercise facility's automated external defibrillator. Some emergency situations may require the evacuation of the exercise facility. In order to lead an evacuation effectively, a fitness instructor needs to know the precise evacuation route.

TERMS OF LITIGATION

The plaintiff is the person who files a lawsuit. The defendant, meanwhile, is the person accused. Many of the cases brought against fitness instructors hinge on the issue of negligence. In basic terms, negligence is the failure to act when action would have prevented injury or damage to the person or property of another. In order for a negligence motion to be filed by a plaintiff, the case must still be within its statute of limitations. The statute of limitations is the length of time within which the state allows for a lawsuit to be filed for a particular offense.

Practice Test

1. The term distal refers to:

   a. Position towards the front of the body
   b. Position towards the back of the body
   c. Position away from the where the limb is attached to the body
   d. Position near where the limb is attached to the body

2. The type of blood vessel that carries blood away from the heart is called:

   a. Vein
   b. Artery
   c. Arteriole
   d. Capillary

3. The function of the trachea is:

   a. Facilitates the passage of food from the mouth to the stomach
   b. Allows air to pass from the larynx into the lungs
   c. Provides a chamber where speech sounds are made in order for talking to occur
   d. Allows for the exchange of respiratory gases

4. All of the following are true about synovial joints EXCEPT:

   a. They are connected to bones with a continuous intervening fibrous tissue
   b. They have a space between the bones that form the joint
   c. They are surrounded by thick, fibrous connective tissue
   d. The surface is lined with a synovial membrane that secretes synovial fluid that acts as a lubricant for the joint

5. What type of motion best describes the rotation for the forearm so the palm of the hand faces upwards?

   a. Inversion
   b. Dorsiflexion
   c. Pronation
   d. Supination

6. The best exercises to work the gluteus maximus would include all of the following EXCEPT:

   a. Straight leg sit ups
   b. Cycling
   c. Jumping rope
   d. Stair climbing

7. Excessive overhead arm motions would most likely result in an injury to:

    a. Biceps brachii
    b. Rotator cuff
    c. Trapezius
    d. Rhomboid major

8. Which of the following would be an appropriate hip flexion strengthening exercise?

    a. Straight leg sit ups
    b. Leg lowering exercises
    c. Using a stability ball, tilting pelvis posteriorly from a supine position
    d. Squats

9. Which of the following conditions would most likely be associated with an older individual with osteoporosis?

    a. Lordosis
    b. Scoliosis
    c. Achondroplasia
    d. Kyphosis

10. Which of the following best describes eccentric movement?

    a. Jogging uphill
    b. Walking down stairs
    c. Doing a sit up
    d. Throwing a ball

11. To assist a client in finding their neutral spine position, which of the following would you most likely recommend?

    a. Finding the middle range when the pelvis is flexed and extended while lying on the floor
    b. Stand up straight and hyperextend the shoulders back
    c. While sitting in a chair, press the small of the back towards the back of the chair, chest forward and lifted
    d. Stand up with knees slightly bent, shoulder blades back, head straight

12. All of the following are true about balance in older adults EXCEPT:

    a. Good balance is extremely important in fall prevention
    b. Balance can be affected by inner ear function or vision
    c. Medications can have a negative impact on balance
    d. A person's ability to balance is predetermined and cannot be improved upon

13. What would be an easy way for a fitness instructor to quickly assess kinesthetic awareness of clients in a fitness class?

    a. Ask each participant to perform a set of bench presses
    b. Observe each participant as they balance on one leg
    c. Observe the movements of participants in the mirror while conducting class
    d. Ask the participant to assess own level of kinesthetic awareness

14. What is the first step a fitness instructor must take in determining appropriate music for a fitness class?

    a. Determine the type of music
    b. Determine the appropriate tempo
    c. Select the appropriate meter
    d. Select the appropriate measure

15. The push up test is used to evaluate all of the following muscles EXCEPT:

    a. Anterior deltoids
    b. Triceps
    c. Quadriceps
    d. Pectoralis major

16. What is the main goal of doing a warm up component for a fitness class?

    a. To raise core body temperature by 1-2° F in order to induce a light sweat
    b. To raise core body temperature by 3° F in order to induce a heavy sweat
    c. To increase the metabolic rate by 10%
    d. To keep core body temperature stable so that the metabolic rate will increase more efficiently during the aerobic component

17. When planning the cardio-respiratory component of a fitness class, all of the following are important considerations EXCEPT:

    a. Demonstrations of the low, medium and high intensity options should be incorporated
    b. Design should include working a variety of muscle groups
    c. A cool down and stretching segment should be planned after the cardio-respiratory component
    d. A low level of intensity should be maintained throughout the work out and participants should adjust their own individual intensity accordingly

18. The benefits of gradually increasing the intensity level of a fitness class include of the following EXCEPT:

    a. The body is better able to redistribute blood flow to the working muscles

    b. The heart normally pumps approximately 5 liters per minute at rest and this rate should gradually increase 10 liters of blood per minute at maximal level during warm up to prevent undue stress

    c. It allows for the diaphragm to gradually warm up thus helping to prevent hyperventilation and side aches from breathing rapidly

    d. It helps the heart to better adjust to changes in intensity during most dangerous periods such as the transition from resting level to high intensity

19. Which of the following best relates the guidelines for static stretching set by the ACSM in 2006?

    a. 1-2 repetitions per muscle group held for 15-30 seconds at least 2-3 days per week

    b. 2-4 repetitions per muscle group held for 30-45 seconds at least 2-3 days per week

    c. 2-4 repetitions per muscle group held for 15-30 seconds at least 2-3 days per week

    d. 2-4 repetitions per muscle group held for 15-30 seconds at least 5 days per week

20. Which of the following is a true statement regarding target heart rate range?

    a. The instructor should advise participants who have heart rates above their target level to make the arm movements smaller and keep feet closer to ground until heart rate lowers to appropriate level

    b. The instructor should be responsible for monitoring heart rates for acceptable ranges

    c. The participant should be responsible for monitoring their own heart rate for acceptable range

    d. Participants should be separated within the class by fitness level to make it easier for the instructor to monitor progress

21. The fitness class you are leading is made up of a wide range of fitness levels. You provide instruction on how to modify the exercises based on fitness level. During the class, you move around the room and provide individual instruction and feedback. What teaching style best illustrates this?

    a. Command style of teaching

    b. Reciprocal style of teaching

    c. Inclusion style of teaching

    d. Practice style of teaching

22. Which of the following would be the most appropriate verbal cue for an exercise class?

    a. "4, 3, 2, 1 leg push out 4 times"
    b. "4, 3, 2, 1 now stay in place knees lift up"
    c. "1, 2, 3, 4 arms reach up"
    d. "1, 2, 3, 4 alternate the arms"

23. What level of intensity of a fitness program is more likely to promote compliance?

    a. Low intensity
    b. Moderate intensity
    c. High intensity
    d. It doesn't matter

24. Which of the following would you be least likely to advise as help to a participant to maintain motivation while missing 2 weeks of exercise classes due to a vacation?

    a. Recommend the participant look for alternative programs at the vacation destination and find out if temporary memberships are available
    b. Encourage the participant to try to be physically active by walking, biking, or any activity that is normally enjoyed
    c. Encourage exercise with family members or friends while on vacation such as morning walk along beach
    d. Recommend shorter, more frequent sessions throughout the day incorporating activities normally enjoyed such as completing three 10 minute walks around the block instead of 30 minutes all at once

25. Which of the following is NOT considered a component of physical fitness?

    a. Muscular strength and endurance
    b. Cardiovascular endurance
    c. Body weight
    d. Flexibility

26. Cardiac output is the product of what two factors?

    a. Heart rate and stroke volume
    b. Stroke volume and blood pressure
    c. Heart rate and pulse
    d. Stroke volume and oxygen consumption

27. What happens when an individual exceeds the anaerobic threshold (AT) during aerobic exercise?

    a. Slight increase in respiratory rate
    b. Steady state is achieved
    c. ATP production begins in the aerobic pathway
    d. Hyperventilation

28. Which of the following would be the best choice of a target zone for exercise intensity level by an elite athlete?

    a. 80% of heart rate reserve
    b. 95% of maximum heart rate
    c. 50% of heart rate reserve
    d. 60% of maximum heart rate

29. When providing advice to a participant about interval training, which of the following would you most likely recommend for a beginner after a 5 minute warm up?

    a. 20 minutes of walking followed by 20 minutes of jogging
    b. 10 minutes of walking followed by 5 minutes of jogging repeat 3 times
    c. 10 minutes of walking followed by 2 minutes of jogging repeat 3 times
    d. 5 minutes of walking followed by 2 minutes of jogging repeat 3 times

30. All of the following are reported benefits of using hand weights while participating in aerobic exercise EXCEPT:

    a. The use of 3-5 pound weight can help to better define the shoulder and upper arm muscles
    b. The use of a 1-3 pound weight can increase heart rate up to 10 beats per minute
    c. The use of 1-3 pound weight can increase caloric expenditure by up to 15%
    d. Hand weights provide a better physiologic response than ankle weights

31. Which of the following is NOT a true statement about the benefits of aerobic activity?

    a. Improvements to the cardio-respiratory system such as a lower heart rate, lower blood pressure and increased maximal oxygen consumption can be attained
    b. Improved bone density through participation in weight bearing exercises which helps reduce the risk for developing osteoporosis
    c. Aerobic exercise helps to prevent insulin resistance by stimulating insulin secretion from the alpha cells in the pancreas. This in turn helps to control blood glucose and potentially delay the long term damage that can be caused by diabetes
    d. Provides assistance with weight control and helps to prevent additional fat stores from being deposited and helps to increase muscle mass. This is turn helps to maintain resting metabolic rate

32. Testosterone is the primary male sex hormone and normal levels can affect all of the following EXCEPT:

    a. Muscle mass
    b. Bone density
    c. Body fat
    d. Cholesterol levels

33. What is the core body temperature that would be indicative of heat stroke?

    a. 106 °F or greater
    b. 105 °F or greater
    c. 104 °F or greater
    d. 103 °F or greater

34. Which of the following would not be considered the best choice of clothing material for exercising in cold weather?

    a. Wool
    b. Gore-Tex
    c. Cotton
    d. Polypropylene

35. Which of the following indicates the proper way to breathe during resistance training?

    a. Exhale during the eccentric phase of the lift and inhale during the concentric phase
    b. Exhale during the concentric phase of the lift and inhale during the eccentric phase
    c. Hold the breath during the lift
    d. Inhale and exhale during both the eccentric and concentric phases of the lift

36. What is the correct energy content per gram for carbohydrate, protein, fat and alcohol?

    a. Carbohydrate 4 kcal/gram, protein 4 kcal/gram, fat 9 kcal/gram, alcohol 7 kcal/gram
    b. Carbohydrate 4 kcal/gram, protein 7 kcal/gram, fat 9 kcal/gram, alcohol 10kcal/gram
    c. Carbohydrate 9 kcal/gram, protein 4 kcal/gram, fat 4 kcal/gram, alcohol 7 kcal/gram
    d. Carbohydrate 4 kcal/gram, protein 4 kcal/gram, fat 9 kcal/gram, alcohol 10 kcal/gram

37. What type of stretching is most likely to stimulate the Golgi tendon organ?

    a. Ballistic
    b. Dynamic
    c. Passive
    d. Static

38. What type of activity will most likely utilize fast twitch muscle fibers?

    a. Walking
    b. Jogging
    c. Sprinting
    d. Swimming

39. Which of the following would not be advisable when teaching a fitness class to a group of older adults that includes a few individuals with a known history of stable coronary heart disease?

    a. Call for Emergency Medical Services immediately if a participant complains of chest pains during class

    b. Allow participants to leave class prior to cool down component

    c. Identify appropriate target heart rate zones based on physician input

    d. Incorporate a longer stretching and warm up component such as light walking or other low intensity exercise prior to moving into higher intensity exercise

40. What is the best beverage to consume for someone who is running 5 miles daily on a treadmill?

    a. Sports drink

    b. Juice

    c. Coffee

    d. Water

41. Viscous or soluble fibers have been shown to help lower blood cholesterol. Which of the following foods is least likely to help with lowering cholesterol?

    a. Cauliflower

    b. Oatmeal

    c. Apples

    d. Kidney beans

42. Fresh fruits and vegetables are encouraged as a main staple in a healthy diet to help prevent cancer and heart disease because they contain:

    a. Vitamin A

    b. Carbohydrates

    c. Insoluble fiber

    d. Phytochemicals

43. Which of the following would be considered a safe amount of weight loss over a 3 month period?

    a. 75 pounds

    b. 25 pounds

    c. 50 pounds

    d. 60 pounds

44. Which of the following would be the most beneficial intervention for a person with type 2 diabetes?

    a. Reduce carbohydrate intake

    b. Increase carbohydrate intake

    c. Achieve a healthy body weight

    d. Increase protein intake

45. Which of the following statements is the least effective way of communicating feedback to a participant?

   a. "Pull your shoulders back and bend your elbows"
   b. "Great job!"
   c. "Put your hands at your temples instead of behind your head"
   d. "Keep your legs straight as you are lowering them"

46. Which of the following characteristics has been identified in participants who are less likely to adhere to a fitness program?

   a. Lower income level
   b. Ethnicity
   c. Previous participation in physical fitness programs
   d. Physical coordination

47. The least desirable characteristic of a group fitness instructor would be:

   a. Taking vacations and periodically switching class with another instructor for variety
   b. Planning class schedules several months ahead
   c. Attending workshops
   d. Starting class on time and carrying class over for a few minutes if participants seem to be motivated and working hard

48. What acronym is helpful to remember when assisting a participant with goal setting?

   a. TRAIN
   b. RICE
   c. SMART
   d. PLAN

49. A new skill becomes a habit in which of the following stages of learning?

   a. Autonomous
   b. Associative
   c. Cognitive
   d. Motivational

50. Which of the following is not a useful strategy in preventing shin splints?

   a. Try not to quickly increase the intensity level from low to high within a class
   b. Allow participants to exercise in bare feet
   c. Encourage lower leg stretching that incorporates the anterior and posterior muscles
   d. Appropriate shock absorbing flooring should be utilized in classes that involve increasing intensity and impact

Answers and Explanations

1. C: There are many terms that describe anatomic positions and these terms usually refer to a complementary structure such as a bone or a muscle. Distal means away from where the limb is attached to the body therefore, the distal radius refers to a location in the forearm close to the wrist. Proximal refers to a position near where the limb is attached to the body. Anterior refers to the front whereas posterior refers to the back. Superior is a term that refers to a position near the head whereas inferior refers to away from the head. Medial describes a position close to the center or midline of the body whereas lateral refers to a position away from the midline. Cervical refers to the area in the neck region. Lumbar refers to the lower back. Plantar refers to the bottom of the foot and dorsal refers to the top of the feet or hands.

2. B: Arteries carry blood away from the heart and veins carry blood to the heart. Arterioles are smaller arteries that branch off from the arteries and bring blood to the smaller vessels known as capillaries. Arteries are thicker and more muscular than veins because the added strength is needed to drive the blood away from the heart. The aorta is the artery that carries oxygenated blood from the heart into circulation. The pulmonary artery carries the oxygen deprived blood back to the lungs. Examples of arteries are the carotid, subclavian, coronary, thoracic, abdominal, brachial, mesenteric, iliac, femoral, popliteal, renal, radial, ulnar, and tibial.

3. B: The respiratory system is the system that supplies oxygen to the body and eliminates carbon dioxide and other waste products from the body. Air enters the body through the nostrils and enters the pharynx. The pharynx is a tubular opening that allows for the passage of food and air. The pharynx leads to the larynx which is the voice box. The trachea follows. This is an approximately 5 inch long tubule that allows air to enter the right or left bronchi. The bronchi further divide into bronchioles which is the location where the exchange of oxygen and carbon dioxide takes place.

4. A: A synovial joint is a joint that moves freely because it has a space between the bones. Thick, fibrous connective tissue surrounds each joint. The inside of the joint is lined with a thin membrane that secretes synovial fluid. This fluid acts to lubricate the joint. Types of synovial joints include gliding joints such as the carpal bones in the wrist, condyloid joints such as the radial carpal joint in the wrist that allows for hand movement, and saddle joints such as the carpal-metacarpal joint in the thumb. Other types include hinge joints such as the elbow, ball and socket joints such as the hip, and pivot joints such as cervical vertebrae nearest the head that allows for a safe range of motion of the head.

5. D: Supination describes the motion of the forearm rotating so the palm is facing upward. It would also apply to the movement of the leg and the foot rolling outward so the foot lands on the outer edge while walking. Pronation is the opposite of

108

supination and refers to the rotation of the hand and forearm so the palm faces downward. Inversion describes the movement of the foot turning inward whereas eversion refers to turning or rotating outward. Dorsiflexion is the movement of the foot upwards towards the shin and plantar flexion refers to the movement of the foot or toes downward toward the sole of the foot. Abduction is any movement away for the midline of the body and adduction is movement towards the midline. Flexion is the bending motion that reduces the angle between two bones such as in the knee. Extension is the unbending motion that increases the angle between two bones such as stretching the knee.

6. A: The gluteus maximus originates at the posterior part of the ilium and sacrum and is the outermost muscle in the buttock region. Extension and external rotation are the primary functions of the muscle. The best exercises to work the gluteus maximus are cycling, stair climbing, squats, and jumping rope. Sit ups done with straight legs would better work the iliacus muscle which originates at the inner edge of the ilium and sacral base. The gluteus medius (middle) and minimus (inner) muscles are also located in the buttocks region and originate at the lateral surface of the ilium. Exercises that best work these muscles would include walking, running or side lying leg raises.

7. B: The rotator cuff muscle originates at the scapula or shoulder and consists of four small muscles. These muscles are called the supraspinatus, infraspinatus, teres minor and subscapularis. They can be remembered with the acronym SITS. The rotator cuff is very important to the overall function of the shoulder joint. It acts to helps stabilize the shoulder joint and allows for free movement. The shoulder is a ball and socket joint with the humeral head (upper portion of the arm) fitting into the shoulder blade (glenoid fossa). Injury to the rotator cuff can be due to an acute reason such as a fall, chronic overuse such as a baseball pitcher or simply due to the aging process. An injury would reduce the ability to abduct the arm or lift the arm up in the air higher than shoulder level. Warming up or stretching before activities that stress the shoulder joint is one way to help prevent injury.

8. C: The primary muscles that facilitate hip flexion include the iliopsoas, rectus femoris, sartorius, and tensor fasciae latae. Since most people have weaker abdominal muscles, straight leg sit ups and leg lowering exercises are not recommended as an exercise to strengthen the hip flexion. This tends to cause hyperextension of the lumbar spine which can result in injury. Squats are an exercise that better work the gluteus maximus and the hamstrings. To strengthen the iliopsoas, the use of a stability ball can help prevent injury. The pelvis can be tilted posteriorly, starting from a supine position, to help with low back stabilization.

9. D: Kyphosis is a disorder of the lumbar spine where there is a well-defined curve in the upper thoracic region. Typically individuals with kyphosis have the appearance of a hunchback where shoulders are rounded, hyperextension of the neck is seen and the chest has a caved or sunken appearance. This is a common disorder in older individuals with osteoporosis. Lordosis is a disorder that is seen in the lower back region and is defined by the buttock area sticking out and the stomach muscles are weakened. Women in the later phase of pregnancy can have this disorder as well as obese individuals with excessive fat around the abdominal area. Scoliosis is where the spine has excessive curving laterally with the appearance of uneven shoulders. Achondroplasia is a congenital condition that causes dwarfism.

10. B: Isotonic muscle contractions involve tension and changes in the length of the muscles in response to tension. Isotonic contractions consist of two types – eccentric and concentric. Eccentric is where the muscle lengthens against a resistance force. An example of this would be walking down stairs where the muscles need to lengthen in order to lower the individual's body weight. Concentric is the opposite and this is where the muscles are shortened such as walking up the stairs where the muscles must contract in order to lift the body weight. Other examples of concentric movement are sit ups, throwing a ball and raising the body up from a squatting position.

11. A: A neutral spine alignment is important in protecting the spine and lower back from injury and stress. The crucial piece of finding a neutral spine is determining the neutral position of the pelvis. This can be accomplished by lying on the floor with knees bent. The pelvic area should be flexed and extended while paying attention to the feeling that occurs with each. A middle range should then be determined by the client. The abdominal muscles should be pulled in flat towards the spine as if trying to balance a cup of water. The spine should be slightly curved away from the floor and not flat on the floor. To achieve a neutral spine while standing, the head should be held straight up with chin in. The shoulder blades should be back with the chest area lifted. The knees should not be bent. The client should pull the abdominal area in towards the spine but the pelvis should not be tilted.

12. D: Balance is important for people of all ages but especially for older adults. As the aging process occurs, the ability to balance diminishes because of reduced muscle strength as well as reduced flexibility. Balance is also affected by inner ear issues as well as vision problems. Many medications can negatively impact balance. Good balance in an older adult is important to performing activities of daily living (ADLs) as well as maintaining independence. Good balance also helps to prevent falls which can lead to injury and even death. Two types of balance are static and dynamic. Static balance is the ability to maintain balance without movement such as standing on one leg. Dynamic balance is maintaining balance while in motion such as walking heel to toe without falling.

13. C: Kinesthetic awareness is the level of self-awareness one has about moving different body parts, and certain parts in coordinated motion. Part of kinesthetic awareness is developing balance, feeling the sensation of muscles flexing and relaxing, and developing good posture. Ballet dancers that perform in a troupe are an example of good kinesthetic awareness. It is not something that can be taught but rather assistance and suggestions can be given to help develop the awareness. One easy way to quickly assess the kinesthetic awareness of a client or class is to teach the class while looking into a mirror. You will be able to tell which participants are able to follow your exact moves easily and which ones cannot.

14. B: Music is an important part of group fitness classes. It helps to provide motivation and enjoyment to those participating. Music is not chosen randomly, but it is carefully selected based on what the instructor is trying to achieve. The first step is determining the appropriate tempo or music speed. This will help set the intensity level of the class. Music that has a slow tempo of less than 100 beats per minute (bpm) is typically used for post stretching. A bpm of 120-140 is used during warm up and cool down. A bpm of 120-160 is generally used for aerobic exercise. Care must be taken in selecting the tempo as rapid tempo means that participants need to move more quickly and are thus at greater risk for injury if they are not used to the tempo and/or movements.

15. C: The push up test is a test commonly conducted to assess upper body strength. The primary muscles that are used during pushups include the anterior and medial deltoids (shoulders), pectoralis major (chest), and triceps (back of upper arm). Once the test is conducted, the results can be compared to results of other people who are of the same age and gender. It is also a useful way to monitor the progress of a participant. Men are tested using the standard position which is hands and toes touching the floor. Women can use the standard position but the data for comparison is based on a modified position where the knees are in contact with the floor instead of the toes.

16. A: The main goal of a proper warm up component to a fitness class is to raise the core body temperature by 1-2 ° F in order to promote a light sweat. A 1° F increase in the core body will increase the metabolic rate by 13%. When the body is warmed up properly, the amount of blood flow to muscles in increased which promotes better energy production in order to better fuel the muscle contractions. Other benefits include improved oxygen exchange between the blood and muscles, relaxation time of the muscle is decreased following the contraction, muscles are more elastic, tendons and ligaments are more flexible and the overall risk for injuries is reduced. The best way to accomplish these benefits is with dynamic movement. This could include a slow jog, arm swings or circles, straight leg kicks, or high knee walk.

17. D: Planning and instructing a group exercise class can be difficult because there are frequently a wide range of abilities within each class. Most participants will select a class based on scheduling rather than intensity level. This can be dangerous if participants are trying to work at a level above their individual ability. Instructors should try to maintain a medium level of intensity and the participants should be advised to work at their own level and pace. Options for a lower and higher intensity version can be incorporated into the design. Class design should incorporate a variety of muscle groups. The class should begin with a warm up segment then a cool down and stretching component should be planned after the cardio-respiratory component. As the class moves through the various components of the class, the instructor should tell the participants what they should be feeling. For example, the

111

participants should be breathing heavily during the peak of the cardio-respiratory portion.

18. B: A gradual increase in intensity is recommended to give the body a chance to adjust physiologically. Blood flow can be redistributed from organ function to the working muscles. It helps the diaphragm warm up to prevent side aches and potential hyperventilation from breathing too quickly due to a too rapid increase in the respiratory rate. It also helps the heart gradually adjust. The heart will normally pump approximately 5 liters of blood per minute at rest. Once maximal peak is attained, the heart can pump up to 30-40 liters of blood per minute. This transition from resting to a maximal working level can be very dangerous for some people.

19. C: Stretching of the major muscle groups is an important part of the flexibility component of the fitness class. The American College of Sports Medicine (ACSM) wrote guidelines in 2006 recommending that static stretches be performed at least 2-3 days per week on the major muscle groups. Two to four repetitions are recommended and the stretch should be held for 15-30 seconds. There are certain precautions that need to be taken during stretching to prevent injury. Bouncing or ballistic stretching is not recommended nor is overstretching of the muscle groups. Participants should be instructed to attain a position where the muscle can be felt as a slight pull then hold. The muscles should not be shaking or vibrating. Correct posture is also a necessity and the instructor should provide verbal reinforcement during the stretching exercise describing proper positioning.

20. A: The instructor and the participant are equally responsible for monitoring heart rates for appropriate levels. The instructor controls the intensity of the workout with the tempo of the music as well as the movements that have been selected. The participant should be advised how to modify the workout out based on heart rate. For example, if the heart rate is above the target level, the participant should reduce the height of leg movements and reduce the size of the arm movements to lower heart rate. Conversely, the participant can increase movements accordingly to increase heart rate closer to target range. Heart rates should be reported in a way that does not demean or threaten any of the participants. This can be done by asking participants to raise hands to indicate if they are above, below or at their target level.

21. D: The practice style of teaching best encompasses a wide range of ability. The instructor can provide basic instruction as well as ways to modify exercises based on ability. The main difference here is that the instructor can observe individuals and provide additional instruction or feedback to maximize skills. The command style of teaching involves the instructor providing direction and expecting immediate response from participants. The ability for individualization is absent. The reciprocal style of teaching uses a partner to help provide feedback to individuals within the class. It is a good style for obtaining fitness assessments. The inclusion style of teaching involves gearing the class to allow for a variety of abilities to help each individual find a level they are comfortable with. The instructor provides alternative exercises when needed to help with this.

22. B: Cueing is an important part of group fitness instruction. It provides a way for participants to follow along and know what is coming next. It is best for the instructor to face the class as often as possible while mirroring techniques such as moving to the left while instructing the class to move to the right. Most appropriate cues will involve body part, action, direction and elaboration. For example, the instructor might tell the group, "Arms reach up double time." It is better to count backwards from 4 rather than to count up from 1. Words that have ambiguous meanings such as "out" should be avoided and replaced with word that have more direct meaning such as up or front. Consistency is key so that the participants get used to your verbal cues. As the instructor, the music level should not be too high to avoid having to shout and sips of water should be taken periodically by the instructor to prevent voice damage.

23. B: Various research studies such as the one done by Perri and colleagues in 2002 have shown that moderate level intensity fitness programs improve compliance to fitness programs. This particular study found that participants of moderate level fitness programs who reached 45-55% of target heart rate reserve were more apt to participate in more sessions and follow prescribed recommendations. The incidence of injury was lower which may also have an impact on compliance. Other factors associated with the program itself that influence compliance are convenient scheduling of classes, class length limited to 60 minutes, and a class that offered a variety to prevent boredom. Compliance is also influenced by how friendly the other participants are as well as the instructor. Environmental issues also play a role such as cleanliness of facility or appropriate temperature level. The level of support is also important as well as how feedback is provided to participants.

24. A: It is inevitable that participants will miss a class or a few classes due to illness, vacation, work or personal schedules. It is important for the instructor to try to encourage continued compliance and adherence to the fitness routine when outside of the class setting. Initiating at least one day of alternative exercise such as walking or biking will help to set the stage for motivation during periods when it is not possible for the participant to attend class. Ideas for participants while on vacation or while not able to attend classes for an extended time include trying to arrange any type of physical fitness activities with a friend or family member such as walking around the block or along the beach. Adding in time during the day for activities that are normally enjoyed such as biking or swimming is also a good way to get exercise. It is also acceptable to break a 30 minute session into three 10 minute sessions.

25. C: Physical fitness is comprised of 5 parts which are muscular strength, muscular endurance, cardiovascular endurance, flexibility and body composition. Body weight is just a small piece of body composition. Body composition includes the amount of lean body mass such as bones, muscles, skin, organs, and certain types of tissue. It also includes adipose tissue or body fat. Adipose tissue is used as a source of energy and is necessary for proper organ function and reproductive issues. A normal range for body fat is 10-13% for women and 2-5% for men. Simply weighing oneself on a scale does not determine body composition. As people age, the amount of body fat naturally increases and the amount of lean body mass will decrease but the actual body weight may not change much.

26. A: Cardiac output is total volume of blood that is pumped by the heart over a certain period of time. This value is typically reported in the amount of liters per minute. Cardiac output is determined by the product of heart rate and stroke volume. Heart rate is the number of heart beats per minute and stroke volume is the amount of blood that is pumped by the left ventricle in each heart beat or contraction. A typical heart can pump approximately 5 liters of blood per minute. As the intensity of exercise increases, the cardiac output can increase as high as 40 liters per minute. An individual's heart rate will increase linearly until the maximum level is reached. Stroke volume, however, tends to increase to approximately 40-50% of the maximum and will then level off. Aerobic exercise helps to strengthen the heart, pump blood more efficiently and increase stroke volume.

27. D: The human body is capable of utilizing many different pathways for energy production. Sometimes the exercise intensity level is so high that the body is not able to keep up with the metabolic demands through the aerobic pathways. A steady state is not able to be achieved and the muscles need to rely on anaerobic pathways to meet the increased demands. When this occurs, the person has reached or exceeded their anaerobic threshold. As this occurs, lactate begins to build up in the blood and the end result is lactic acid. Continuation of exercise at this point is very difficult and hyperventilation and cramping often result.

28. B: Generally accepted intensity levels are 40-85% of heart rate reserve or 60-95% of maximum heart rate. The heart rate is the number of beats per minute and the heart rate reserve is the difference between the maximal heart rate and the resting heart rate of an individual. Maximal heart rate can be determined by exercise testing or by using a predictive equation. A rule of thumb to determine maximal heart rate is to subtract age from 220. An elite athlete will typically be able to tolerate a higher level of maximal heart rate whereas unconditioned or less fit individuals should work at a lower level initially until the fitness level improves.

29. D: Interval training is alternating high and low levels of intensity during exercise sessions. High intensity level involves increasing maximal heart rate to 80-100% for a short period of time ranging from 10 seconds up to 5 minutes. Low intensity level involves allowing the heart rate to slow down and is considered a recovery or rest period. For a beginner who does not usually jog, it is best to use a lower time frame initially. After a 5 minute warm up involving walking at a slow pace, the rest set will begin. Five minutes is a good target to start with followed by a work set of 2 minutes of jogging. This should be repeated 3 times for a total workout of 26 minutes. The schedule can be adjusted as the fitness level improves.

30. A: The addition of hand weights is a frequent choice to try to increase the intensity of a workout. Wrist weights are the preferred choice over hand weights because the gripping of the hand weights can cause an elevation of blood pressure in certain individuals. The use of 1-3 pound weights is also preferred because weights heavier than 3 pounds can cause too much strain on the shoulder and arm muscles and may cause injury. Using 1-3 pound weights can increase heart rate by up to 10 beats per minute. There is also a 5-15% increase in caloric expenditure as well as oxygen consumption by using 1-3 pound weights. Hand weights provide a better advantage over ankle weights by increasing heart rate more. Ankle weights can also cause issues with movement in the lower extremities and may have a higher risk of injury.

31. C: Aerobic exercise is beneficial in so many ways. It helps to strengthen and improve the cardio-respiratory system but lowering blood pressure and heart rate, increasing stroke volume which is the amount of blood pumped with each heartbeat, helps to increase oxygen consumption and helps overall to increase lung capacity. Bone density is also a favorable affected especially with weight bearing exercise. This in turn helps to prevent or delay osteoporosis after the age of 50. Aerobic exercise also helps to limit additional fat stores from being formed and helps to increase lean body mass. The preservation of lean body mass helps to keep the resting metabolic rate steady. Aerobic exercise also helps with blood glucose control. Exercise helps prevent insulin resistance by increasing the efficiency of insulin. Insulin is secreted by beta cells in response to a glucose load.

32. D: Testosterone is the primary male sex hormone. It is produced and released by the testes in males and is also produced by the ovaries in females. Testosterone has both androgenic and anabolic effects. The androgenic effects include the development of male characteristics such as facial hair and changes in facial structure. The anabolic effects include muscle development. It also helps with bone development and with body weight. Normal levels of testosterone do not increase cholesterol levels. When individuals take testosterone or other anabolic steroids to try to increase muscle mass, they run the risk of developing side effects such as high cholesterol levels, development of breasts in men, decrease in testicular size, and acne.

33. B: Exercising in heat and humidity can be very dangerous. During exercise under normal conditions, the body produces sweat to help dissipate the heat. As the sweat accumulates on the skin, it is evaporated which helps to cool the skin. When the temperature level and/or humidity increase, the body is less able to regulate this. The heart rate is increased more than usual and the amount of sweating increases the risk for dehydration. The symptoms of heat exhaustion include a core body temperature less than or equal to 104 ° F, a weakened pulse, hypotension, nausea, overall weakness, extreme sweating and clammy feeling skin. Heat stroke occurs when the core body temperature exceeds 105 ° F. Symptoms include skin that is flushed and bright red, a strong pulse that is beating rapidly, and difficulty breathing. The individual should stop exercising, assistance should be given to try to immediately cool the body and medical help should be obtained.

34. C: The difficulties with exercising in extreme cold weather are brought about by an increased loss of body heat which can potentially lead to frostbite or hypothermia. Exercising in the cold can cause vasoconstriction which can be dangerous for individuals with heart disease. The recommendations for exercising in the cold include wearing several layers of clothing, changing clothing when it becomes wet or sweaty, and selecting the appropriate type of clothing. Cotton is a good choice of fabric in hot weather because it allows for the evaporation of sweat; however, because it tends to soak up the sweat, it is not a good choice to wear in the cold weather. Better choices of fabric include Gore-Tex or polypropylene. Nylon is a good selection for outer wear because it helps to repel the wind.

35. B: Concentric and eccentric contractions are opposite. To illustrate the difference, when lifting weights, the lifting part is considering concentric while the lowering component is eccentric. To breathe properly when doing any type of resistance training, the individual should be instructed to inhale during the eccentric or lowering component and exhale during the concentric or lifting portion. It is extremely important to breathe properly. Many individuals will hold their breath while lifting. When this occurs, the glottis can close which can cause an increase in pressure in the chest area. This increase in pressure can impact the proper blood flow back to the heart resulting in less blood to pump. This may lead to feeling dizzy or even fainting because f the lack of oxygen delivery to the brain. This is called the Valsalva maneuver.

36. A: Energy or calories (kcal) are derived from food in the forms of macronutrients and alcohol. Macronutrients include carbohydrates, protein, and fat. Carbohydrates contribute 4 kcal/gram and are in the form of simple carbohydrates such as table sugar or sweets or complex carbohydrate such as whole grain breads or pasta. Protein contributes 4 kcal/gram. It is important to consume sufficient protein so it is not used as a caloric source but rather can be used for repair of tissues, building cells and muscles, production of enzymes and hormones, and building immune function. Fat is calorically dense at 9 kcal/gram and consist of saturated fats such as butter or meat fat and unsaturated fat such as vegetable oils. Alcohol does not contribute any nutrition to the body beside calories because it is not a good source of vitamins or minerals. Alcohol is also calorically dense at 7 kcal/gram.

37. D: The Golgi tendon organ (GTO) is a sensory organ that is located within a tendon that helps with muscle tension. Static stretching is the type of stretching most likely to stimulate the GTO. Static stretching is done by holding a stretch. There is no bouncing or pulling. A static stretch should be held for 30 seconds to a minute. Holding for less than 30 seconds does not allow the muscle to relax completely. When the stretch is done without any movement as in a static stretch, the GTO sends a message to the muscle spindle to lengthen the muscle causing the muscles to stretch and relax. This helps to prevent injury to the muscles and ligaments. This is especially important when a muscle is overstretched causing the muscle contraction to stop.

38. C: Muscles are comprised of fast twitch and slow twitch fibers. Each type of fiber utilizes a different metabolic pathway to get energy. Fast twitch fibers utilize anaerobic metabolism and are used mainly for movements that are quick and intense such as sprinting or jumping. They are better able to fuel activities that require short bursts of energy. Slow twitch muscle fibers utilize aerobic metabolism. They are better able to fuel lower intensity activities that last a longer time such as jogging or walking. Athletes that run marathons or triathlons will most likely utilize slow twitch muscle fibers. The type of muscle fibers each individual has within their body is determined by genetics although slow twitch muscle fibers will respond to training better than fast twitch muscle fibers.

39. B: Coronary heart disease causes the most deaths for both men and women in the United States. When teaching a fitness class, there is a great likelihood that at least one participant will carry that diagnosis. Individuals with advanced coronary heart disease should be referred to a cardiac rehabilitation program where close monitoring is available by qualified professionals. Individuals with stable coronary heart disease should participate in a longer warm up and stretching component before higher intensity exercise is initiated. If any chest pain or discomfort is felt at any time during the class, Emergency Medical Services should be called immediately. If the individual experiences other types of symptoms such as dizziness, this should be communicated to the physician. The individual's physician should provide advice on proper target heart rate and blood pressure ranges and no individual should leave the class or fitness center prior to their heart rate and blood pressure returning to resting levels.

40. D: Adequate hydration is essential for anyone participating in any type of exercise. The majority of the time, water is the best beverage to hydrate the body and quench thirst. The kidneys function to regulate fluid and electrolyte balance. If a person is exercising strenuously for more than an hour, a sports drink is acceptable. Caffeinated drinks and alcohol are not acceptable choices for hydration because both act as a diuretic in the body. Most people can use thirst as a gauge for hydration. General guidelines for hydration during exercise are to drink approximately 500-600 ml of fluid before starting exercise. During exercise, 200-300 ml of fluid should be consumed every 10-20 minutes. After completion of exercise, body weight can be obtained. For every 0.5 kg of body weight lost, approximately 500 ml of fluid should be consumed to replace lost fluids.

41. A: There are two main types of fiber – soluble fiber (also called viscous fiber) and insoluble fiber (also called incompletely fermented fiber). Soluble fiber has been shown to help lower blood cholesterol levels because it helps to reduce absorption of dietary cholesterol by the body. Foods that are high in soluble fiber include oatmeal, oat bran, peas, citrus fruits, and the pulp of an apple. Insoluble fiber is more beneficial in the digestive process and elimination. This type of fiber is not completely digested. Foods that contain insoluble fiber include wheat cereal and bread, and certain vegetables such as Brussels sprouts, cabbage, and cauliflower. Both types of fiber should be consumed every day. The Dietary Reference Intake

(DRIs) recommends 38 grams of fiber each day for men under the age of 50 and 25 grams per day for women under the age of 50. For those older than 50, the recommendations are 30 grams for men and 21 grams for women.

42. D: Fresh fruits and vegetables are nature's way of assisting in disease prevention. In addition to the many vitamins and minerals they contain, fruits and vegetables are also a rich source of phytochemicals and antioxidants. Tomatoes contain lycopene which is thought to help prevent prostate and lung cancer. Certain berries such blueberries and strawberries are thought to block the growth of early cancer causing cells. Dark green leafy vegetables such as collards, turnips and spinach contain lutein and zeaxanthin that are believed to assist cells in resisting free radical damage. Cruciferous vegetables such as cauliflower, broccoli and cabbage are especially important because they are thought to boost immune function. It is much better to consume these foods as part of a healthy diet rather than to take a supplement.

43. B: Obesity is a common problem in the United States for both adults and children. There are several factors that contribute to this problem including excessive calorie intake, diets that are high in fat, lack of physical activity, and genetics. To lose 1 pound of body fat, an individual must burn 500 calories per day over and above what is consumed. A safe level of weight loss is approximately 2 pounds per week so over a 3 month period; 25 pounds would be approximately 2 pounds per week. Rates higher than this may not be safe and may not be associated with long term success in keeping the weight off. Initial weight loss may be higher in the first week or so due to fluid fluctuations. Using a very low calorie or starvation diet can be dangerous. The best way to lose weight is to cut out some high calorie foods and to increase physical activity.

44. C: Individuals who are overweight or obese have an increased risk for developing type 2 diabetes. The most beneficial intervention for anyone with type 2 diabetes is weight loss. Achieving and maintaining an ideal body weight is essential in reducing blood glucose levels, as well as delaying or preventing the many complications that can arise from diabetes. Even a 5-10% weight loss can have a dramatic effect on blood glucose levels. Complications such as vision impairment, numbness or tingling in the extremities, heart disease, kidney disease, and issues with skin healing can all be exacerbated by poorly controlled diabetes. A registered dietitian can assist individuals with meal planning and weight loss. Complex carbohydrates should be consumed over simple carbohydrates. Foods high in fiber should also be incorporated as well as healthy fats. Incorporating physical activity into daily life is also a key point in achieving and maintaining an appropriate body weight.

45. B: There are a few effective ways of providing feedback. One way is to be specific about what the participant is doing correctly or incorrectly. Simply saying "Great job" does not indicate to the participant what they are doing correctly. Another way to provide feedback is to give information such as "Put your hands at your temples instead of behind your head" when doing sit ups. Once the behavior is corrected, it can be followed up with positive reinforcement such as "That's the way". Providing immediate feedback is important so the participant can relate to what you are trying to say. If feedback is not immediate, the behavior may not be corrected appropriately. Feedback should always be delivered gently and never in a confrontational or mean spirited way. If several members of the group are doing the same incorrect behavior, it is better to address the group rather than to pick out individuals.

46. A: Individuals who smoke, are overweight, or of lower income or socioeconomic status, are less likely to adhere or comply with a physical fitness program or routine. Qualities that make an individual more likely to comply include those who have good time management skills, can deal with stress effectively, can enjoy exercise and not perceive it in a negative fashion, and have the self confidence that they can accomplish something. The best way to find out this type of information is to have participants complete a questionnaire or to interview the person as they join a group. It will provide insight into possible compliance level at the start. Special attention can be paid to those individuals identified as high risk for dropping out especially for those who are participating in a class with multiple skill levels. Utilizing the ratings of perceived exertion (RPE) scale is one way to help address this to help prevent overexertion by the high risk participant.

47. D: The choice for least desirable characteristic of a group fitness instructor would be carrying class over for a few minutes. Classes should start and end on time because participants have other commitments and find it helpful to follow a schedule. Providing a schedule for several months in advance is very helpful especially when holidays or other closings are indicated in advance. It is important for a group fitness instructor to be dependable and to refrain from frequent unplanned absences if at all possible. Dedication is a good trait and this can be demonstrated by obtaining appropriate certifications and attending workshops to keep the knowledge base up to date. Instructors should help take responsibility for proper functioning of the facility such as alerting the proper person to help fix something or get an issue taken care of rather than ignoring it. Taking regular vacations and occasionally switching classes with another instructor can help to prevent burn out.

48. C: Goal setting can be difficult but is important in the physical fitness process. It is a way to gauge progress in a measurable way. The acronym SMART is helpful when assisting a participant with goal setting. S stands for specific which is the what, where, when and with whom questions that need to be answered. The M stands for measurable and this points to the importance of determining when a goal has been concretely met such as setting a specific heart rate goal. A stands for attainable. This is simply setting reasonable goals. A beginner in an exercise program should not set a goal of participating in a high intensity kick boxing class on their first day at the program. R stands for relevant which means the goal should be specific to the individual's situation and T stands for time-bound which answers the questions how often, for how long and how soon.

49. A: Three stages of learning as related to motor skills were described in 1967 by Paul Fitts and Michael Posner. The first stage is the cognitive stage. In this stage, the individual is trying to learn a new skill but makes errors and the skill is not consistent. Correct breathing can be an issue in this stage. The second stage is called the associative stage. In this stage, the skill becomes more consistent and the individual is less likely to make errors. Most of the time, the individual is also able to recognize when the skill is not being performed correctly. The third stage is the autonomous stage. It is in this stage that the new skill becomes a habit. The individual is performing the skill without needing to think about what is being done, but is still able to recognize when mistakes are made. Driving a car is an example of a skill done in this stage.

50. B: Shin splints are a common injury caused mainly through overuse by repetitive motions of the lower leg such as from running. The foot is not able to adequately absorb the impact of the shock and this can lead to micro tearing of the anterior and posterior muscles in the lower leg. Proper footwear is essential is helping to prevent shin splints and orthotics are sometimes prescribed for individuals who are prone to this injury. Continuous repetitive movement on hard surfaces is discouraged and appropriate flooring that helps to absorb shock is recommended for classes with increased intensity or impact. Individuals should be encouraged to adequately stretch their lower leg muscles including the anterior and posterior muscles. If an individual has a shin splint, proper treatment includes ice and rest followed by stretching and strengthening of the lower legs.

How to Overcome Test Anxiety

Just the thought of taking a test is enough to make most people a little nervous. A test is an important event that can have a long-term impact on your future, so it's important to take it seriously and it's natural to feel anxious about performing well. But just because anxiety is normal, that doesn't mean that it's helpful in test taking, or that you should simply accept it as part of your life. Anxiety can have a variety of effects. These effects can be mild, like making you feel slightly nervous, or severe, like blocking your ability to focus or remember even a simple detail.

If you experience test anxiety—whether severe or mild—it's important to know how to beat it. To discover this, first you need to understand what causes test anxiety.

Causes of Test Anxiety

While we often think of anxiety as an uncontrollable emotional state, it can actually be caused by simple, practical things. One of the most common causes of test anxiety is that a person does not feel adequately prepared for their test. This feeling can be the result of many different issues such as poor study habits or lack of organization, but the most common culprit is time management. Starting to study too late, failing to organize your study time to cover all of the material, or being distracted while you study will mean that you're not well prepared for the test. This may lead to cramming the night before, which will cause you to be physically and mentally exhausted for the test. Poor time management also contributes to feelings of stress, fear, and hopelessness as you realize you are not well prepared but don't know what to do about it.

Other times, test anxiety is not related to your preparation for the test but comes from unresolved fear. This may be a past failure on a test, or poor performance on tests in general. It may come from comparing yourself to others who seem to be performing better or from the stress of living up to expectations. Anxiety may be driven by fears of the future—how failure on this test would affect your educational and career goals. These fears are often completely irrational, but they can still negatively impact your test performance.

> **Review Video: 3 Reasons You Have Test Anxiety**
> Visit mometrix.com/academy and enter code: 428468

121

Elements of Test Anxiety

As mentioned earlier, test anxiety is considered to be an emotional state, but it has physical and mental components as well. Sometimes you may not even realize that you are suffering from test anxiety until you notice the physical symptoms. These can include trembling hands, rapid heartbeat, sweating, nausea, and tense muscles. Extreme anxiety may lead to fainting or vomiting. Obviously, any of these symptoms can have a negative impact on testing. It is important to recognize them as soon as they begin to occur so that you can address the problem before it damages your performance.

> **Review Video: 3 Ways to Tell You Have Test Anxiety**
> Visit mometrix.com/academy and enter code: 927847

The mental components of test anxiety include trouble focusing and inability to remember learned information. During a test, your mind is on high alert, which can help you recall information and stay focused for an extended period of time. However, anxiety interferes with your mind's natural processes, causing you to blank out, even on the questions you know well. The strain of testing during anxiety makes it difficult to stay focused, especially on a test that may take several hours. Extreme anxiety can take a huge mental toll, making it difficult not only to recall test information but even to understand the test questions or pull your thoughts together.

> **Review Video: How Test Anxiety Affects Memory**
> Visit mometrix.com/academy and enter code: 609003

Effects of Test Anxiety

Test anxiety is like a disease—if left untreated, it will get progressively worse. Anxiety leads to poor performance, and this reinforces the feelings of fear and failure, which in turn lead to poor performances on subsequent tests. It can grow from a mild nervousness to a crippling condition. If allowed to progress, test anxiety can have a big impact on your schooling, and consequently on your future.

Test anxiety can spread to other parts of your life. Anxiety on tests can become anxiety in any stressful situation, and blanking on a test can turn into panicking in a job situation. But fortunately, you don't have to let anxiety rule your testing and determine your grades. There are a number of relatively simple steps you can take to move past anxiety and function normally on a test and in the rest of life.

> **Review Video: How Test Anxiety Impacts Your Grades**
> Visit mometrix.com/academy and enter code: 939819

Physical Steps for Beating Test Anxiety

While test anxiety is a serious problem, the good news is that it can be overcome. It doesn't have to control your ability to think and remember information. While it may take time, you can begin taking steps today to beat anxiety.

Just as your first hint that you may be struggling with anxiety comes from the physical symptoms, the first step to treating it is also physical. Rest is crucial for having a clear, strong mind. If you are tired, it is much easier to give in to anxiety. But if you establish good sleep habits, your body and mind will be ready to perform optimally, without the strain of exhaustion. Additionally, sleeping well helps you to retain information better, so you're more likely to recall the answers when you see the test questions.

Getting good sleep means more than going to bed on time. It's important to allow your brain time to relax. Take study breaks from time to time so it doesn't get overworked, and don't study right before bed. Take time to rest your mind before trying to rest your body, or you may find it difficult to fall asleep.

> **Review Video: The Importance of Sleep for Your Brain**
> Visit mometrix.com/academy and enter code: 319338

Along with sleep, other aspects of physical health are important in preparing for a test. Good nutrition is vital for good brain function. Sugary foods and drinks may give a burst of energy but this burst is followed by a crash, both physically and emotionally. Instead, fuel your body with protein and vitamin-rich foods.

Also, drink plenty of water. Dehydration can lead to headaches and exhaustion, especially if your brain is already under stress from the rigors of the test. Particularly if your test is a long one, drink water during the breaks. And if possible, take an energy-boosting snack to eat between sections.

> **Review Video: How Diet Can Affect your Mood**
> Visit mometrix.com/academy and enter code: 624317

Along with sleep and diet, a third important part of physical health is exercise. Maintaining a steady workout schedule is helpful, but even taking 5-minute study breaks to walk can help get your blood pumping faster and clear your head. Exercise also releases endorphins, which contribute to a positive feeling and can help combat test anxiety.

When you nurture your physical health, you are also contributing to your mental health. If your body is healthy, your mind is much more likely to be healthy as well. So take time to rest, nourish your body with healthy food and water, and get moving as much as possible. Taking these physical steps will make you stronger and more able to take the mental steps necessary to overcome test anxiety.

Mental Steps for Beating Test Anxiety

Working on the mental side of test anxiety can be more challenging, but as with the physical side, there are clear steps you can take to overcome it. As mentioned earlier, test anxiety often stems from lack of preparation, so the obvious solution is to prepare for the test. Effective studying may be the most important weapon you have for beating test anxiety, but you can and should employ several other mental tools to combat fear.

First, boost your confidence by reminding yourself of past success—tests or projects that you aced. If you're putting as much effort into preparing for this test as you did for those, there's no reason you should expect to fail here. Work hard to prepare; then trust your preparation.

Second, surround yourself with encouraging people. It can be helpful to find a study group, but be sure that the people you're around will encourage a positive attitude. If you spend time with others who are anxious or cynical, this will only contribute to your own anxiety. Look for others who are motivated to study hard from a desire to succeed, not from a fear of failure.

Third, reward yourself. A test is physically and mentally tiring, even without anxiety, and it can be helpful to have something to look forward to. Plan an activity following the test, regardless of the outcome, such as going to a movie or getting ice cream.

When you are taking the test, if you find yourself beginning to feel anxious, remind yourself that you know the material. Visualize successfully completing the test. Then take a few deep, relaxing breaths and return to it. Work through the questions carefully but with confidence, knowing that you are capable of succeeding.

Developing a healthy mental approach to test taking will also aid in other areas of life. Test anxiety affects more than just the actual test—it can be damaging to your mental health and even contribute to depression. It's important to beat test anxiety before it becomes a problem for more than testing.

Review Video: Test Anxiety and Depression
Visit mometrix.com/academy and enter code: 904704

Study Strategy

Being prepared for the test is necessary to combat anxiety, but what does being prepared look like? You may study for hours on end and still not feel prepared. What you need is a strategy for test prep. The next few pages outline our recommended steps to help you plan out and conquer the challenge of preparation.

STEP 1: SCOPE OUT THE TEST

Learn everything you can about the format (multiple choice, essay, etc.) and what will be on the test. Gather any study materials, course outlines, or sample exams that may be available. Not only will this help you to prepare, but knowing what to expect can help to alleviate test anxiety.

STEP 2: MAP OUT THE MATERIAL

Look through the textbook or study guide and make note of how many chapters or sections it has. Then divide these over the time you have. For example, if a book has 15 chapters and you have five days to study, you need to cover three chapters each day. Even better, if you have the time, leave an extra day at the end for overall review after you have gone through the material in depth.

If time is limited, you may need to prioritize the material. Look through it and make note of which sections you think you already have a good grasp on, and which need review. While you are studying, skim quickly through the familiar sections and take more time on the challenging parts. Write out your plan so you don't get lost as you go. Having a written plan also helps you feel more in control of the study, so anxiety is less likely to arise from feeling overwhelmed at the amount to cover.

STEP 3: GATHER YOUR TOOLS

Decide what study method works best for you. Do you prefer to highlight in the book as you study and then go back over the highlighted portions? Or do you type out notes of the important information? Or is it helpful to make flashcards that you can carry with you? Assemble the pens, index cards, highlighters, post-it notes, and any other materials you may need so you won't be distracted by getting up to find things while you study.

If you're having a hard time retaining the information or organizing your notes, experiment with different methods. For example, try color-coding by subject with colored pens, highlighters, or post-it notes. If you learn better by hearing, try recording yourself reading your notes so you can listen while in the car, working out, or simply sitting at your desk. Ask a friend to quiz you from your flashcards, or try teaching someone the material to solidify it in your mind.

STEP 4: CREATE YOUR ENVIRONMENT

It's important to avoid distractions while you study. This includes both the obvious distractions like visitors and the subtle distractions like an uncomfortable chair (or a too-comfortable couch that makes you want to fall asleep). Set up the best study environment possible: good lighting and a comfortable work area. If background music helps you focus, you may want to turn it on, but otherwise keep the room quiet. If you are using a computer to take notes, be sure you don't have any other windows open, especially applications like social media, games, or anything else that could distract you. Silence your phone and turn off notifications. Be sure to keep water close by so you stay hydrated while you study (but avoid unhealthy drinks and snacks).

Also, take into account the best time of day to study. Are you freshest first thing in the morning? Try to set aside some time then to work through the material. Is your mind clearer in the afternoon or evening? Schedule your study session then. Another method is to study at the same time of day that you will take the test, so that your brain gets used to working on the material at that time and will be ready to focus at test time.

STEP 5: STUDY!

Once you have done all the study preparation, it's time to settle into the actual studying. Sit down, take a few moments to settle your mind so you can focus, and begin to follow your study plan. Don't give in to distractions or let yourself procrastinate. This is your time to prepare so you'll be ready to fearlessly approach the test. Make the most of the time and stay focused.

Of course, you don't want to burn out. If you study too long you may find that you're not retaining the information very well. Take regular study breaks. For example, taking five minutes out of every hour to walk briskly, breathing deeply and swinging your arms, can help your mind stay fresh.

As you get to the end of each chapter or section, it's a good idea to do a quick review. Remind yourself of what you learned and work on any difficult parts. When you feel that you've mastered the material, move on to the next part. At the end of your study session, briefly skim through your notes again.

But while review is helpful, cramming last minute is NOT. If at all possible, work ahead so that you won't need to fit all your study into the last day. Cramming overloads your brain with more information than it can process and retain, and your tired mind may struggle to recall even previously learned information when it is overwhelmed with last-minute study. Also, the urgent nature of cramming and the stress placed on your brain contribute to anxiety. You'll be more likely to go to the test feeling unprepared and having trouble thinking clearly.

So don't cram, and don't stay up late before the test, even just to review your notes at a leisurely pace. Your brain needs rest more than it needs to go over the information again. In fact, plan to finish your studies by noon or early afternoon the day before the test. Give your brain the rest of the day to relax or focus on other things, and get a good night's sleep. Then you will be fresh for the test and better able to recall what you've studied.

STEP 6: TAKE A PRACTICE TEST

Many courses offer sample tests, either online or in the study materials. This is an excellent resource to check whether you have mastered the material, as well as to prepare for the test format and environment.

Check the test format ahead of time: the number of questions, the type (multiple choice, free response, etc.), and the time limit. Then create a plan for working through them. For example, if you have 30 minutes to take a 60-question test, your limit is 30 seconds per question. Spend less time on the questions you know well so that you can take more time on the difficult ones.

If you have time to take several practice tests, take the first one open book, with no time limit. Work through the questions at your own pace and make sure you fully understand them. Gradually work up to taking a test under test conditions: sit at a desk with all study materials put away and set a timer. Pace yourself to make sure you finish the test with time to spare and go back to check your answers if you have time.

After each test, check your answers. On the questions you missed, be sure you understand why you missed them. Did you misread the question (tests can use tricky wording)? Did you forget the information? Or was it something you hadn't learned? Go back and study any shaky areas that the practice tests reveal.

Taking these tests not only helps with your grade, but also aids in combating test anxiety. If you're already used to the test conditions, you're less likely to worry about it, and working through tests until you're scoring well gives you a confidence boost. Go through the practice tests until you feel comfortable, and then you can go into the test knowing that you're ready for it.

Test Tips

On test day, you should be confident, knowing that you've prepared well and are ready to answer the questions. But aside from preparation, there are several test day strategies you can employ to maximize your performance.

First, as stated before, get a good night's sleep the night before the test (and for several nights before that, if possible). Go into the test with a fresh, alert mind rather than staying up late to study.

Try not to change too much about your normal routine on the day of the test. It's important to eat a nutritious breakfast, but if you normally don't eat breakfast at all, consider eating just a protein bar. If you're a coffee drinker, go ahead and have your normal coffee. Just make sure you time it so that the caffeine doesn't wear off right in the middle of your test. Avoid sugary beverages, and drink enough water to stay hydrated but not so much that you need a restroom break 10 minutes into the test. If your test isn't first thing in the morning, consider going for a walk or doing a light workout before the test to get your blood flowing.

Allow yourself enough time to get ready, and leave for the test with plenty of time to spare so you won't have the anxiety of scrambling to arrive in time. Another reason to be early is to select a good seat. It's helpful to sit away from doors and windows, which can be distracting. Find a good seat, get out your supplies, and settle your mind before the test begins.

When the test begins, start by going over the instructions carefully, even if you already know what to expect. Make sure you avoid any careless mistakes by following the directions.

Then begin working through the questions, pacing yourself as you've practiced. If you're not sure on an answer, don't spend too much time on it, and don't let it shake your confidence. Either skip it and come back later, or eliminate as many wrong answers as possible and guess among the remaining ones. Don't dwell on these questions as you continue—put them out of your mind and focus on what lies ahead.

Be sure to read all of the answer choices, even if you're sure the first one is the right answer. Sometimes you'll find a better one if you keep reading. But don't second-guess yourself if you do immediately know the answer. Your gut instinct is usually right. Don't let test anxiety rob you of the information you know.

If you have time at the end of the test (and if the test format allows), go back and review your answers. Be cautious about changing any, since your first instinct tends to be correct, but make sure you didn't misread any of the questions or accidentally mark the wrong answer choice. Look over any you skipped and make an educated guess.

At the end, leave the test feeling confident. You've done your best, so don't waste time worrying about your performance or wishing you could change anything. Instead, celebrate the successful completion of this test. And finally, use this test to learn how to deal with anxiety even better next time.

> **Review Video: 5 Tips to Beat Test Anxiety**
> Visit mometrix.com/academy and enter code: 570656

Important Qualification

Not all anxiety is created equal. If your test anxiety is causing major issues in your life beyond the classroom or testing center, or if you are experiencing troubling physical symptoms related to your anxiety, it may be a sign of a serious physiological or psychological condition. If this sounds like your situation, we strongly encourage you to seek professional help.

Thank You

We at Mometrix would like to extend our heartfelt thanks to you, our friend and patron, for allowing us to play a part in your journey. It is a privilege to serve people from all walks of life who are unified in their commitment to building the best future they can for themselves.

The preparation you devote to these important testing milestones may be the most valuable educational opportunity you have for making a real difference in your life. We encourage you to put your heart into it—that feeling of succeeding, overcoming, and yes, conquering will be well worth the hours you've invested.

We want to hear your story, your struggles and your successes, and if you see any opportunities for us to improve our materials so we can help others even more effectively in the future, please share that with us as well. **The team at Mometrix would be absolutely thrilled to hear from you!** So please, send us an email (support@mometrix.com) and let's stay in touch.

> **If you'd like some additional help, check out these other resources we offer for your exam:**
> **http://MometrixFlashcards.com/GroupFitness**

Additional Bonus Material

Due to our efforts to try to keep this book to a manageable length, we've created a link that will give you access to all of your additional bonus material:

mometrix.com/bonus948/acegroupfitins